Student Loan Forgiveness
or Ten Years to Life?

STUDENT LOAN FORGIVENESS or TEN YEARS TO LIFE?

A Responsible Visual Guide to Your Federal Student Loan Repayment Options

DANE SPANCAKE,
Federal Student Loan Counselor, MBA—Finance

Copyright © 2016 Dane A. Spancake.

All rights reserved. No part of this book may be used or reproduced by any means, graphic, electronic, or mechanical, including photocopying, recording, taping or by any information storage retrieval system without the written permission of the author except in the case of brief quotations embodied in critical articles and reviews.

Archway Publishing books may be ordered through booksellers or by contacting:

Archway Publishing
1663 Liberty Drive
Bloomington, IN 47403
www.archwaypublishing.com
1 (888) 242-5904

Because of the dynamic nature of the Internet, any web addresses or links contained in this book may have changed since publication and may no longer be valid. The views expressed in this work are solely those of the author and do not necessarily reflect the views of the publisher, and the publisher hereby disclaims any responsibility for them.

Any people depicted in stock imagery provided by Thinkstock are models, and such images are being used for illustrative purposes only.
Certain stock imagery © Thinkstock.

ISBN: 978-1-4808-2891-9 (sc)
ISBN: 978-1-4808-2892-6 (hc)
ISBN: 978-1-4808-2893-3 (e)

Library of Congress Control Number: 2016905917

Print information available on the last page.

Archway Publishing rev. date: 04/13/2017

DEDICATION

I dedicate this book to my mother and father.

To my mother, who, even on her worst days in her fight with cancer, always found the time to ask me, "How is your book coming along?" But, she was quick to counter any answers with "Shouldn't you be done with it by now?" This is my mom!

To my father, who assures that the math inside is accurate.

I thank both for their lifelong support whether I succeeded or I failed.

CONTENTS

Preface ix

Chapter 1: The Basics. 1

Chapter 2: Traditional Repayment Plans 25
The Standard Ten-Year (Fixed) Plan 26
The Graduated Ten-Year Plan 32
Extended-Year Repayment Schedules 35

Chapter 3: Income-Driven Repayment—The Rage! 41
Pay As You Earn (PAYE). 52
Revised Pay As You Earn (REPAYE) 55
Income-Based Repayment (IBR) 57
Income-Contingent Repayment (ICR). 59
Income-Sensitive (IS). 66

Chapter 4: Teacher Loan Forgiveness. 69

Chapter 5: Public Service Loan Forgiveness 76

Chapter 6: Deferment and Forbearance—A Borrower's
              Privilege?. 87

Chapter 7: Parent PLUS Loans—"Thank You, Mom and Dad!" 102

Chapter 8: Direct Consolidation—Only If You Must!.... 119

Chapter 9: Your Credit Score—You Control It! 128

Conclusion 131

Notes 133

PREFACE

Congratulations! You have succeeded in the goal that you had established for yourself: you have graduated from college. You now comprise the 32 percent of the American population that holds a bachelor's degree or higher.[1] Now is the time to explore the multiple options presented to you as you enter the repayment stage on your student loan debt. This book will provide you a pathway to best understand the finance (in easy-to-understand methodologies and analysis) behind the different repayment choices that await you, given the amount of your student loan debt, your current income, or your overall personal situation. Of course, these choices may also bring headwinds that may take you off course occasionally from your original plans.

The following chapters will explore the monetary consequences of your choices, bad luck, or good fortunes. If you have had lingering questions since your exit from school, you will find that this book seeks to close the many gaps that exist in the information-gathering process you will face from your first payment to your last. The order of the chapters has relevance. The student loan industry is predicated on your ability to be a responsible borrower. With this in mind, the sequence of the chapters dealing with loan repayment choices follows the exact hierarchy recommended by the industry, from the shortest payback period (ten years) to the longest (thirty years). Only you, the borrower, can determine the option that's right for you. The US Congress will continue to tinker from time to time with the repayment model, but we, as Americans, know that the decision to pursue a post-secondary education comes with costs and that the burden of student loan repayment rests on our own shoulders … and should not necessarily rest on the shoulders of others!

CHAPTER 1

The Basics

> In our democracy every young person should have an opportunity to obtain a higher education regardless of his station in life or financial means.
> —President John F. Kennedy (liberal Democrat), 1962

You now owe on federal student loans. Perhaps up to your neck, or worse, your eyeballs! Now is the time to better understand these loans—to know how they all work. You deserve it!

We begin with the basics.

We have all seen the student loan calculator projection tools that provide answers such as "Over ten years your estimated total interest paid is $x.xx and your estimated total principal paid is $y.yy." Project too far into the future, even five years, and the numbers prove meaningless. For most of us, anytime the horizon stretches beyond the upcoming weekend, or beyond the next sports season, it is way too far in the future to have any *real* relevance—let alone ten or even twenty-five years in the future. My suggestion: Forget these silly projection exercises. Simply concentrate on one daily figure. This daily figure is referred to commonly as the *daily interest accrual*.

The Daily Interest Accrual Formula

Daily Interest (*i*) Accrual = (Loan *i* rate/100) / # days in the year x loan balance

What's *your* daily interest cost figure? Is it less than one dollar? Or is it between one and five dollars, six and ten dollars, eleven and twenty dollars, twenty-one and thirty dollars, or higher yet? As a responsible student loan borrower, you need to uncover this daily figure. If the daily cost grows too large, you will have to pay that much more money over time to bring it back down. You should walk around each day with this one simple figure in your head. Learn it. But, more importantly, respect its relevance.

For example, suppose Sam graduated with a bachelor of science degree in engineering in May. Sam looks at his student loan portfolio dated November 15—the end date of his six-month grace period. It reads as follows (assumes a full disbursement):

Loan Type	Disbursement	Original Bal.	Current Bal.	*i* Rate	Outstanding *i*	Payoff
DLUNST	08/15/2014	$2,000.00	$2,000.00	4.66%	$114.25	$2,114.25
DLSTFD	08/15/2014	$5,500.00	$5,500.00	4.66%	$0.00	$5,500.00
DLUNST	08/18/2013	$2,000.00	$2,000.00	3.86%	$172.20	$2,172.20
DLSTFD	08/18/2013	$5,500.00	$5,500.00	3.86%	$106.72	$5,606.72
DLUNST	08/20/2012	$2,000.00	$2,000.00	6.80%	$438.45	$2,438.45
DLSTFD	08/20/2012	$4,500.00	$4,500.00	3.40%	$75.44	$4,575.44
DLUNST	08/15/2011	$2,000.00	$2,000.00	6.80%	$575.35	$2,575.35
DLSTFD	08/15/2011	$3,500.00	$3,500.00	3.40%	$0.00	$3,500.00
Total		$27,000.00	$27,000.00		$1,482.41	$28,482.41

Notice that Sam's original principal balance (the original amount he borrowed to attend school) is exactly the same total as his current principal balance (the original balance plus any

THE BASICS

outstanding interest that has been capitalized). In December, Sam receives an *interest notice* that reads something like this:

This is not a bill:

Pay by: December 20, 2015
Total Interest Due: $1,482.41

If you elect to not pay this amount by December 20, 2015, the interest will capitalize (added to your original balance). You will then pay a fixed rate of interest on this higher loan balance.

Note: Your installment bill (standard ten-year fixed repayment schedule) has already been calculated by the time you receive the above notice. If you elect to pay the above interest amount, it *will not* decrease your installment bill! Instead, your installment bill will simply *not* increase.

If Sam elects to pay all his interest before he enters repayment, his daily interest accrual figure for all his student loans remains at $3.21 a day. Here are the calculations:

Direct Loan Unsubsidized Stafford (DLUNST): (4.66/100)/365 x $2,000 = $0.25 (no rounding).
Direct Loan Subsidized Stafford (DLSTFD): (4.66/100)/365 x $5,500 = $0.70.
Direct Loan Unsubsidized Stafford (DLUNST): (3.86/100)/365 x $2,000 = $0.21.
Direct Loan Subsidized Stafford (DLSTFD): (3.86/100)/365 x $5,500 = $0.58.
Direct Loan Unsubsidized Stafford (DLUNST): (6.80/100)/365 x $2,000 = $0.37.
Direct Loan Subsidized Stafford (DLSTFD): (3.40/100)/365 x $4,500 = $0.41 (no rounding).
Direct Loan Unsubsidized Stafford (DLUNST): (6.80/100)/365 x $2,000 = $0.37.

Direct Loan Subsidized Stafford (DLSTFD): (3.40/100)/365 x $3,500 = $0.32 (no rounding).
Sam's total daily interest accrual figure equals $3.21 per day.

Note: Congress temporarily eliminated the grace period interest subsidy for Federal Direct Loan Program (FDLP) subsidized loans made on or after July 1, 2012, and before July 1, 2014, as a result of a budget impasse.[2]

If Sam elects not to pay any of his $1,482.41 of outstanding interest before his December 20 interest notice due date, his interest will *capitalize* (interest outstanding is added to the original principal balance to create a new larger balance referred to as the *current principal balance*). Interest will no longer accrue daily on his original principal balance, but rather interest will now accrue daily on Sam's larger *current principal balance*. See the illustration (below):

After interest capitalization:

Loan Type	Disbursement	Original Bal.	Current Bal.	i Rate	Outstanding i	Payoff Bal.
DLUNST	08/15/2014	$2,000.00	$2,114.25	4.66%	$9.00	$2,123.25
DLSTFD	08/15/2014	$5,500.00	$5,500.00	4.66%	$25.20	$5,525.20
DLUNST	08/18/2013	$2,000.00	$2,172.20	3.86%	$7.56	$2,179.76
DLSTFD	08/08/2013	$5,500.00	$5,606.72	3.86%	$20.88	$5,627.60
DLUNST	08/20/2012	$2,000.00	$2,438.45	6.80%	$13.32	$2,451.77
DLSTFD	08/20/2012	$4,500.00	$4,575.44	3.40%	$14.76	$4,590.20
DLUNST	08/15/2011	$2,000.00	$2,575.35	6.80%	$13.32	$2,588.67
DLSTFD	08/15/2011	$3,500.00	$3,500.00	3.40%	$11.52	$3,511.52
Total		$27,000.00	$28,482.41		$115.56	$28,597.97

Sam's new total daily interest calculation is:
Direct Unsubsidized (DLUNST): (4.66/100)/365 x $2,114.25 = $0.27.
Direct Subsidized (DLSTFD): (4.66/100)/365 x $5,500 = $0.70.

THE BASICS

Direct Unsubsidized (DLUNST): (3.86/100)/365 x $2,172.20 = $0.23.
Direct Subsidized (DLSTFD): (3.86/100)/365 x $5,606.72 = $0.59.
Direct Unsubsidized (DLUNST): (6.80/100)/365 x $2,438.45 = $0.45.
Direct Subsidized (DLSTFD): (3.40/100)/365 x $4,575.44 = $0.42 (no rounding).
Direct Unsubsidized (DLUNST): (6.80/100)/365 x $2,575.35 = $0.48.
Direct Subsidized (DLSTFD): (3.40/100)/365 x $3,500 = $0.32 (no rounding).
Sam's new total daily interest accrual figure increases to $3.46 per day.

Now imagine for a moment a daily interest accrual figure that exceeds fifty dollars, seventy-five dollars, or one hundred dollars and more a day. Ouch! How does this happen? Too many postponed payment periods and capitalization-of-interest events!

Notice, also, that Sam still has an outstanding interest balance on his loan portfolio ——— thirty-six days to be exact (his accrued interest from November 16, through December 20). If Sam's first installment was due on December 20, and if he made his first installment payment on this same date or later, a disproportionate amount of his first installment payment (regardless of whether he paid his interest notice amount of $1,482.41 or not) would be applied to cover these thirty-six days of accrued interest. (The hierarchy of federal student loan payment application is fees first, outstanding interest second, and principal last.) Next month, however, if Sam made his January payment on the twentieth or sooner, a greater amount of his January installment payment would be applied to principal, since he had fewer days of interest accrual (twenty-nine days or less) between his current payment and his last payment (assume December 20).

Note: Even this simple exercise is tedious and time-consuming. You may simply call your federal loan servicer—appointed to service your loan by the US Department of Education at loan origination—to obtain your personal daily interest figure. Trust me, you will impress the representative who entertains your call.

Who Determines the Interest Rate on Federal Student Loans?
Congress sets the interest rate on all disbursed Federal Direct Loan Program (FDLP) loans.[3] Congress had also set the interest rates on the now discontinued Federal Family Education Loans (FFEL) (issued prior to 2013) but with little to no adjustments to the fixed rate of interest from year to year. In 2010, the Health Care and Education Reconciliation Act changed the federal student loan model in the United States and granted the US government 100 percent control. Now the federal government, through FDLP, issues *all* federal loans to students and parents.[4] The act forced the banks out of the federal student loan issuance business and discontinued the entire FFEL Program, where banks and Wall Street played middlemen.

On what authority?
The Bipartisan Student Loan Certainty Act of 2013 gives Congress the authority to establish the interest rate on *newly disbursed* Federal Direct Loan Program (FDLP) loans for the upcoming school year.[5]

Note: If you have had a loan disbursed in a prior year, your interest rate has already been cemented contractually. Its stated interest rate will remain fixed for the life of the loan.

Officially, the new rates are announced on July 1 of every year.[6] This official interest rate announcement is one of two important annual government releases that are closely watched in the student loan industry. As a borrower, you may wish to know why these releases are important.

U.S. Congress Official FDLP Interest Rate Announcement:	
When:	**Every July 1**
Who:	**U.S. Congress**
Why it's Important:	It establishes the interest rates in effect on newly disbursed federal student loans for the upcoming school year. This interest rate will remain fixed over the life of the loan.

Source: https://studentaid.ed.gov/about/announcements/interest-rate

The above release is the official interest rate announcement for the upcoming school year. However, you may calculate the "unofficial interest rate" months in advance of the official announcement. Below is an explanation.

How does Congress set the new interest rates?

When the US. government raises (borrows) money to fund its operations throughout the year and beyond, it does so by issuing US Treasury securities at auctions. The US Treasury conducts these auctions on a scheduled basis. The government has no money, in theory, so it must borrow money just like you, the student. According to the excerpt from the act (below), the results of one particular treasury auction will influence your interest cost to borrow in the upcoming school year and throughout the life of your loan:

> "The 10-year Treasury auction in the most recent month prior to a June 1 cutoff date."[7]

The US Treasury security auction schedule is patterned each year according to type of instrument as follows:

U.S. Treasury Auction Pattern	
Type of Note	Frequency of Auction
2-year	Monthly
3-year	Monthly
5-year	Monthly
7-year	Monthly
10-year	Original Issues: February, *May,* August and November

Source: https://www.treasurydirect.gov/instit/instit.htm?upcoming

To locate the tentative ten-year Treasury Note Auction calendar, visit https://www.treasurydirect.gov/instit/annceresult/annceresult.htm

One may quickly decipher, according to the above auction schedule, the May auction (an original issue auction) *must be* the one that will consistently influence your next school year's student loan borrowing (interest) rates. Unless, of course, the government suddenly has little need to borrow more money—an unlikely event, indeed!

In 2015, the auction held on May 13 met the guidelines as "the most recent month prior to a June 1 cutoff date" established in the Bipartisan Student Loan Certainty Act of 2013.

On the subsequent two pages are the Official US Treasury Auction Announcement and the Official Results as released, within approximately fifteen minutes after the auction closed, by the Department of the Treasury's Bureau of the Fiscal Service.

STUDENT LOAN FORGIVENESS OR TEN YEARS TO LIFE?

TREASURY NEWS

Department of the Treasury • Bureau of the Fiscal Service

Embargoed Until 08:30 A.M.
May 06, 2015

CONTACT: Treasury Securities Services
202-504-3550

TREASURY OFFERING ANNOUNCEMENT [1]

Term and Type of Security	10-Year Note
Offering Amount	$24,000,000,000
Currently Outstanding	$0
CUSIP Number	912828XB1
Auction Date	May 13, 2015
Original Issue Date	May 15, 2015
Issue Date	May 15, 2015
Maturity Date	May 15, 2025
Dated Date	May 15, 2015
Series	C-2025
Yield	Determined at Auction
Interest Rate	Determined at Auction
Interest Payment Dates	November 15 and May 15
Accrued Interest from 05/15/2015 to 05/15/2015	None
Premium or Discount	Determined at Auction
Minimum Amount Required for STRIPS	$100
Corpus CUSIP Number	912820U96
Additional TINT(s) Due Date(s) and	None
CUSIP Number(s)	None
Maximum Award	$8,400,000,000
Maximum Recognized Bid at a Single Yield	$8,400,000,000
NLP Reporting Threshold	$8,400,000,000
NLP Exclusion Amount	$0
Minimum Bid Amount and Multiples	$100
Competitive Bid Yield Increments [2]	0.001%
Maximum Noncompetitive Award	$5,000,000
Eligible for Holding in TreasuryDirect®	Yes
Estimated Amount of Maturing Coupon Securities Held by the Public	$67,026,000,000
Maturing Date	May 15, 2015
SOMA Holdings Maturing	$1,448,000,000
SOMA Amounts Included in Offering Amount	No
FIMA Amounts Included in Offering Amount [3]	Yes
Noncompetitive Closing Time	12:00 Noon ET
Competitive Closing Time	1:00 p.m. ET

[1] Governed by the Terms and Conditions set forth in The Uniform Offering Circular for the Sale and Issue of Marketable Book-Entry Treasury Bills, Notes, and Bonds (31 CFR Part 356, as amended), and this offering announcement.
[2] Must be expressed as a yield with three decimals e.g., 7.123%.
[3] FIMA up to $1,000 million in noncompetitive bids from Foreign and International Monetary Authority not to exceed $100 million per account.

THE BASICS

TREASURY NEWS

Department of the Treasury • Bureau of the Fiscal Service

For Immediate Release
May 13, 2015

CONTACT: Treasury Securities Services
202-504-3550

TREASURY AUCTION RESULTS

Term and Type of Security	10-Year Note
CUSIP Number	912828XB1
Series	C-2025
Interest Rate	2-1/8%
High Yield [1]	2.237%
Allotted at High	96.52%
Price	99.001405
Accrued Interest per $1,000	None
Median Yield [2]	2.220%
Low Yield [3]	2.190%
Issue Date	May 15, 2015
Maturity Date	May 15, 2025
Original Issue Date	May 15, 2015
Dated Date	May 15, 2015

	Tendered	Accepted
Competitive	$65,248,625,000	$23,950,105,000
Noncompetitive	$46,264,900	$46,264,900
FIMA (Noncompetitive)	$4,000,000	$4,000,000
Subtotal [4]	**$65,298,889,900**	**$24,000,369,900** [5]
SOMA	$542,818,600	$542,818,600
Total	**$65,841,708,500**	**$24,543,188,500**

	Tendered	Accepted
Primary Dealer [6]	$39,924,000,000	$4,535,000,000
Direct Bidder [7]	$7,393,000,000	$5,004,000,000
Indirect Bidder [8]	$17,931,625,000	$14,411,105,000
Total Competitive	**$65,248,625,000**	**$23,950,105,000**

---

[1] All tenders at lower yields were accepted in full.
[2] 50% of the amount of accepted competitive tenders was tendered at or below that yield.
[3] 5% of the amount of accepted competitive tenders was tendered at or below that yield.
[4] Bid-to-Cover Ratio: $65,298,889,900/$24,000,369,900 = 2.72
[5] Awards to TreasuryDirect = $30,397,900.
[6] Primary dealers as submitters bidding for their own house accounts.
[7] Non-Primary dealer submitters bidding for their own house accounts.
[8] Customers placing competitive bids through a direct submitter, including Foreign and International Monetary Authorities placing bids through the Federal Reserve Bank of New York.

Yes, this reads $24 billion.

To locate the ten-year treasury note high-yield auction results, visit: http://www.treasurydirect.gov/instit/annceresult/press/press_secannpr.htm

Why the US Treasury ten-year note?
The US Treasury ten-year note is one of the most important, most liquid, and most widely watched interest rate indicators in the world. This rate serves as the primary indicator of the health of the US economy, and it serves as a proxy to which most other interest rates are pegged, such as a fixed-rate mortgage. And now you can add your federal student loan to this list! Many factors influence the interest rate set on this debt instrument. For the simple purpose of this book, the most significant factors are the strength of the US economy and the perception around the world that the US government will be able to meet its future debt obligations. There is little fear around the globe that the US government will ever default on its debt, for the simple reason that the United States is one of only four countries in the world that can print money and the US Congress can simply raise its debt ceiling ever higher to allow for future increased borrowing.[8] This is not without limitations, however. According to the World Bank analysis, there is a consequential tipping point that a country may reach when its debt levels rise above a 75-plus percent ratio for an extended period of time (i.e., decades versus only a few years).[9] Currently, the US debt ratio stands at 100 percent, which means that the US government is already leveraged to the equivalent of one full year of US economic output[10] (the US economy stood at $17.4 trillion in 2014[11]).

A Brief Summary of the 2015 Results for the Ten-Year Treasury Note Auction

On May 13, 2015, the US government (seller/borrower) offered $24 billion of ten-year treasury notes to its potential buyers (lenders) in exchange for a promise to pay a stated rate (coupon rate) of interest of 2⅛ percent (2.125 percent or .02125) for the next ten years. (This coupon rate of 2⅛ percent is determined by the implied yield on notes already traded in the marketplace, rounded up to the nearest one-eighth of a percentage point to allow for the bond to be auctioned closer to its par-value or $1,000.00.) Demand for the notes exceeded the available supply by a robust margin of 2.72 to 1 (bid to cover); in other words, there was $2.72 of buyer/lender dollars for every one dollar of notes up for sale.

However, the US government accepted 96.52 percent of orders at a discount to the $1,000.00 face value it guarantees to repay on the notes in ten years. Lenders (buyers of the notes) were only willing to pay $990.01 (99.001405 x 10 = $990.01405). The lenders, on this day, were primarily foreign governments, such as Japan and China—the indirect bidders at 60.7 percent—who drove the effective yield higher (the high yield) to 2.237 percent on a discounted purchase price. This is where you, the student loan borrower, enter.

The New Federal Direct Loan Program (FDLP) Student Loan Interest Rate Formula

As set forth under the Bipartisan Student Loan Certainty Act of 2013, borrowing rates on *all* new Federal Direct Loan Program (FDLP) loan originations are calculated by the formula below:

Final Rate	=	High Yield Rate	+	Add-on Rate

Source: HR1911—Bipartisan Student Loan Certainty Act of 2013

What is a high-yield rate?

The high-yield rate is the highest interest rate level achieved at the Treasury auction—the best rate possible to the buyer (lender). However, it is the *worst rate* for the U.S. Government as the borrower, and more importantly, for you as the student or the parent as a borrower of the U.S. Government. Below is the exact language in the act:

> The high-yield rate "is equal to the high yield that is reached during the 10-year Treasury auction in the most recent month prior to a June 1 cutoff date."

The U.S. Government—your new student loan banker—asks you, to help it pay back this high-yield rate differential with a little extra interest on your student loans! In the above auction example, the extra interest cost to you is .112 percent or $1.12 (2.237 percent - 2.125 percent = .112 percent x 1,000 = $1.12) in additional interest payments per every $1,000.00 of student loans you borrow to attend school in calendar year 2015–2016. In theory, the higher rate of interest you must pay based on the *high yield* will fund the coffers of foreign central banks (indirect bidders), mutual fund investment houses (direct bidders), and Wall Street investment house trading accounts (twenty-two primary dealers in total, such as Goldman Sachs and Morgan Stanley)[12] and provides a nice income check to wealthy individuals (indirect bidders as ... *the savers*)!

THE BASICS

The government asks you to pay the highest interest rate—*"the high yield rate"*—that is reached during the bidding process at auction.

Below is the short, four-year history of ten-year note Treasury auction outcomes that transpired in the month of May from 2013 to 2016 following the passage of the new act.

	10- Year Treasury Note Recent Auction Results (Prior to a June 1, cut-off date)				
Auction Date	Total Amt. ($ Bill.)	Coupon Rate (%)	Bid/ Cover Ratio	High Yield (%)	% Allotted at High Yld (%)
May-11-2016	$23.00	1.625	2.68	1.710	30.57
May-13-2015	$24.00	2.125	2.72	2.237	96.52
May-7-2014	$24.00	2.5	2.63	2.612	82.17
May-8-2013	$24.00	1.75	2.70	1.810	94.12

The Add-On Rate

The add-on rate is a constant in the above Direct Loan Program interest rate formula. This rate is a profit cushion (an additional interest rate spread) that Congress has decided to charge you, the student or parent of an undergraduate student, to borrow from it. It is nothing but an arbitrary figure, a mere first guesstimate by Congress so it may cover its administrative costs to service your loan (through approved federal loan servicers), and protect it against the risk of defaults. These extra interest costs imposed on you will also help fund the *expansion* of this massive new student loan entitlement program, the Federal Direct Loan Program (FDLP). Below are the fixed *add-on* rates that Congress has set in the act. Students and parents of undergraduate students have paid these extra add-on rates since the beginning of the 2014 school year.

New Direct Loan Add-on Rates		
Direct Loan Type	Loan Code	Issued On or After Oct, 1 2014 & beyond
Direct Loan Subsized Stafford	DLSTFD	2.050%
Direct Loan Unsubsidized Stafford	DLUNST	
Direct Loan Unsubsidized Stafford – Graduate or professional	DLUNST	3.600%
Direct Loan PLUS – Graduate or professional	DLPLGB	4.600%
Direct Loan PLUS – Parent (The parent is the loan holder)	DLPLUS	

Source: HR1911—Bipartisan Student Loan Certainty Act of 2013

The Final Rate

Simply add the *high-yield* rate (a variable) and the *add-on* rate (a constant) together and you have your final loan rate *(rounded to the nearest hundredth or .00)* as follows:

Final Direct Loan Rates (July 1, 2015 and before July 1, 2016)						
Loan Type	Loan Code	High Yield Rate	(+)	Add-On Rate	=	Final Rate
Direct Loan Subsized Stafford	DLSTFD	2.237%	(+)	2.05%	=	4.29%
Direct Loan Unsubsized Stafford	DLUNST	2.237%	(+)	2.05%	=	4.29%
Direct Loan Unsubsized – Graduate or professional	DLUNST	2.237%	(+)	3.60%	=	5.84%
Direct Loan PLUS – Graduate or professional	DLPLGB	2.237%	(+)	4.60%	=	6.84%
Direct Loan PLUS – Parent	DLPLUS	2.237%	(+)	4.60%	=	6.84%

Source: https://studentaid.ed.gov/types/loans/interest-rates#who-sets-interest-rates-for-federal-student-loans

During the 2015 school year, a student borrower of direct loans, both subsidized and unsubsidized (DLSTFD and DLUNST), paid an interest rate of 4.29 percent. This rate of interest is a 101 percent markup on the coupon rate the US government must pay of 2⅛ percent (i.e., 2.125 percent) on its own debt, the ten-year treasury note auctioned on May 13, 2015. For parent borrowers through the Direct PLUS loan program for parents of undergraduate students, it's an even higher markup of 221 percent. Yikes!

How high may interest rates rise on new federal student loans?
Under the act, Congress has imposed interest rate caps. These caps depend on your level of educational pursuit—undergraduate school or graduate school—and whether or not you or a parent are the borrower. The new direct loan rate caps set by Congress are as follows:

THE BASICS

New Direct Loan Interest Rate Caps		
Direct Loan Type	Loan Code	Interest Rate Caps
Direct Loan Subsized Stafford	DLSTFD	8.25%
Direct Loan Unsubsidized Stafford	DLUNST	8.25%
Direct Loan Unsubsidized Stafford – Graduate or professional	DLUNST	9.50%
Direct Loan PLUS – Graduate or professional	DLPLGB	10.50%
Direct Loan PLUS – Parent	DLPLUS	10.50%

Source: HR1911—Bipartisan Student Loan Certainty Act of 2013

We may rearrange the formula to determine the highest high-yield rate possible at a future auction that will trigger the above interest rate caps for a direct loan borrower:

Final Rate (Cap)	-	Add-on Rate	=	High Yield Rate (Trigger)

Undergraduates 8.25% - 2.05% = 6.20%
Graduate 9.50% - 3.60% or 10.50% - 4.60% = 5.90%
Parent borrowers 10.50% - 4.60% = 5.90%

Keep in mind that the historical average yield for the ten-year treasury note, from the period January 1963 to March 2015, was 6.66 percent, well above these trigger rates:

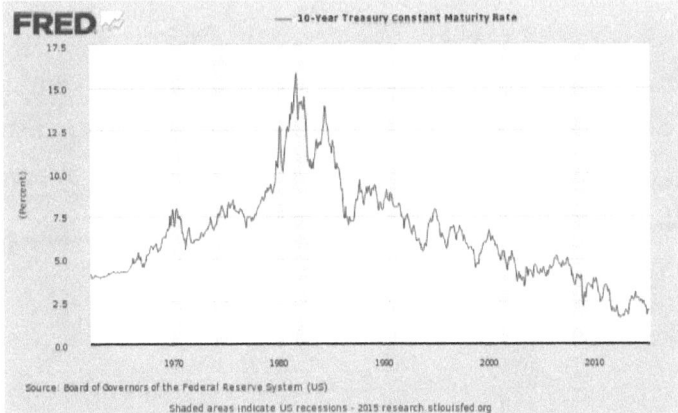

Source: http://learnbonds.com/historical-treasury-yields-2-year-bill-10-year-note-30-year-bond/8546/

The second most important government announcement is:

The Annual Federal Poverty Guidelines

Federal Poverty Guidelines Release:	
When:	Every year, before or after the 3rd week in January
Who:	U.S. Department of Health and Human Services (HHS)
Why it is important:	It sets the earnings guidelines (based on family size and state of residency) to prove financial hardship. These earnings guidelines (after adjustments in some instances) are used to determine borrower eligibility for certain types of deferments, and income-driven repayment (IDR) plan types.

Source: HHS.gov

Every January, on or about the fifteenth of the month, the Department of Health and Human Services (HHS) issues its annual poverty guidelines that determine the basic income level an individual or a large family must have in order to provide the essentials of life—food, shelter, and clothing. There are three different sets of poverty guidelines according to where you reside: the forty-eight contiguous states plus Washington DC, Alaska, and Hawaii. We hear you Boston, Chicago, Los Angeles, Manhattan, and San Francisco! Sorry, but your cost of living allowance is considered no different. Below is an historical chart that lists the most recent releases compared to calendar year 2000.

THE BASICS

Health and Human Services (HHS) Poverty Guidelines (selected years):

48 CONTIGUOUS STATES AND WASHINGTON, D.C.

Persons in family/household	2017	2016	2015	2014	2013	2000
1	$12,060	$11,880	$11,770	$11,670	$11,490	$8,350
2	$16,240	$16,020	$15,930	$15,730	$15,510	$11,250
3	$20,420	$20,160	$20,090	$19,790	$19,530	$14,150
4	$24,600	$24,300	$24,250	$23,850	$23,550	$17,050
5	$28,780	$28,440	$28,410	$27,910	$27,570	$19,050
6	$32,960	$32,580	$32,570	$31,970	$31,590	$22,850
7	$37,140	$36,730	$36,730	$36,030	$35,610	$25,750
8	$41,320	$40,890	$40,890	$40,090	$39,630	$28,650

*For families/households with more than 8 persons, add $4,180 for each additional person in 2017, $4,160 in 2016, $4,160 in 2015, $4,060 in 2014, $4,020 in 2013 and $2,900 in 2000.

ALASKA

Persons in family/household	2017	2016	2015	2014	2013	2000
1	$15,060	$14,840	$14,720	$14,580	$14,350	$10,430
2	$20,290	$20,020	$19,920	$19,660	$19,380	$14,060
3	$25,520	$25,200	$25,120	$24,740	$24,410	$17,690
4	$30,750	$30,380	$30,320	$29,820	$29,440	$21,320
5	$35,980	$35,560	$35,520	$34,900	$34,470	$24,950
6	$41,210	$40,740	$40,720	$39,980	$39,500	$28,580
7	$46,440	$45,920	$45,920	$45,060	$44,530	$32,210
8	$51,670	$51,120	$51,120	$50,140	$49,560	$35,840

*For families/households with more than 8 persons, add $5,230 for each additional person in 2017, $5,200 in 2016, $5,200 in 2015, $5,080 in 2014, $5,030 in 2013 and $3,630 in 2000.

HAWAII

Persons in family/household	2017	2016	2015	2014	2013	2000
1	$13,860	$13,670	$13,550	$13,420	$13,230	$9,590
2	$18,670	$18,430	$18,330	$18,090	$17,850	$12,930
3	$23,480	$23,190	$23,110	$22,760	$22,470	$16,270
4	$28,290	$27,950	$27,890	$27,430	$27,090	$19,610
5	$33,100	$32,710	$32,670	$32,100	$31,710	$22,950
6	$37,910	$37,470	$37,450	$36,770	$36,330	$26,290
7	$42,720	$42,230	$42,230	$41,440	$40,950	$29,630
8	$47,530	$47,010	$47,010	$46,110	$45,570	$32,970

*For families/households with more than 8 persons, add $4,810 for each additional person in 2017, $4,780 in 2016, $4,780 in 2015, $4,670 in 2014, $4,620 in 2013, and $3,340 in 2000.

Source: HHS.gov

As you can see, the numbers do not change dramatically from year to year. This release provides the base numbers to determine one's eligibility for financial hardship deferments and forbearances or lower payments on certain income-driven repayment (IDR) plans. In most instances, the above numbers are adjusted by a factor of 150 percent (an exception is Income-Contingent Repayment at 100 percent). There is more on this topic in chapters 3 and 6.

The Two Major Federal Student Loan Programs

The William D. Ford Federal Direct Loan Program (FDLP) and the now defunct Federal Family Education Loan (FFEL) Program are the two major categories of federal student loan programs. Most of you only need to concern yourself with one type, the FDLP. For others who attended school prior to the 2008 school year, you may have been issued loans under the old FFEL program.

What is the difference?

The Two Major Types of Federal Loan Programs	
Federal Direct Loan Program (FDLP)*	**Loan Code**
Direct Loan Subsidized Stafford	DLSTFD
Direct Loan Unsubsidized Stafford	DLUNST
Direct Loan Unsubsidized Stafford – Graduate or professional students	DLUNST
Direct Loan PLUS – Graduate or professional students	DLPLGB
Direct Loan PLUS – Parent	DLPLUS
* FDLP was introduced as early as 1992	
Federal Family Education Loan (FFEL)* Program	
Subsidized Stafford	STFD
Unsubsidized Stafford	UNSTFD
Unsubsidized Stafford – Graduate or professional students	UNSTFD
Plus – Graduate or professional students	PLUSGB
Plus – Parent	PLUS
* FFEL was discontinued in 2008	

Federal Direct Loan Program (FDLP):
These loans are issued directly by the federal government through the Department of Education. These loans are direct federal government guaranteed issues, and therefore, the taxpayer is now at *100 percent risk* in the event of borrower default. As highlighted earlier, the Obama administration's enactment of the Health Care and Education Act of 2010 seized 100 percent control of the federal student loan lending model and forced the banks out along with the FFEL program. Under this new congressional mandate, *all* federal government loan issuance will now be conducted through the Department of Education's new Direct Loan Program.

THE BASICS

The new *"EXPANSIONARY"* Federal Direct Loan Program (FDLP) funding model:

U.S. Taxpayer – risk increased to 100% in the event of student loan default.

US Treasury

US Congress

Title IV Participant Schools

US Department of ED

Title IV Additional Servicers (TIVAS)

Students & Parents of Students

Third Parties – Fee for service
Why pay a fee to consolidate your student loans or change the repayment plan terms on your student loans? Simply call your Department of Ed, assigned, Title IV Additional Servicer (TIVA) or visit the Federal Student Aid website *www.student loans.gov* and do-it-yourself... its easy and its free!

Federal Family Education Loan (FFEL) Program:

These loans originated from the funds of private institutions (i.e., commercial banks, state-funded organizations, etc.). The government paid these private institutions' fees to originate and administer the loans, which provided a steady stream of income to the issuing institution. As a borrower paid off a loan, capital was now available to issue a new loan to another eager borrower ... and the cycle was repeated. These institutions were willing to risk their capital on student loans on the basis of the federal government stepping in and making whole on the loan in the event of borrower default. Ultimately, taxpayer risk was *limited*.

The original *"RESTRICTIVE"* Federal Family Education Loan *(*FFEL) Program funding model:

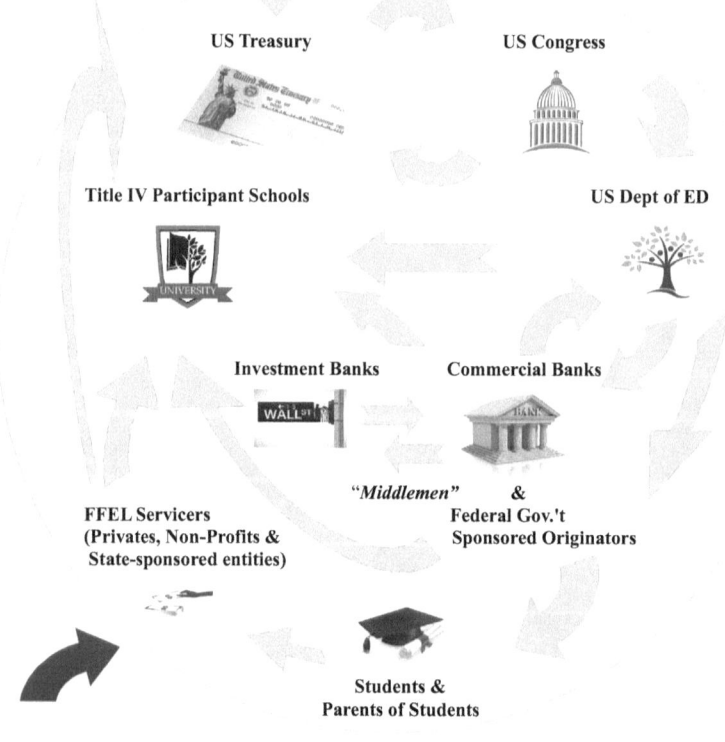

Source: Department of Ed

Who services my loan?

The Department of Education assigns you a federal loan servicer the moment your loan is disbursed. Your loan servicer's customer service mission is mandated by Congress to offer assistance and guidance—as your trusted advisor—as you pay on your loan. A key point of emphasis is, *none* of the Department of Education assigned loan servicers will charge you a fee on *most* activities involving the servicing of your FDLP loan or any older FFEL loan that has been purchased by the Department. "This includes: repayment plan selection and loan consolidation."[13] The current list of federal loan servicers that have been awarded contracts are:

Department of ED Federal Loan Servicers			
NSLDS Federal Loan Servicer Listings	Tax Status	Telephone #	Website
Original "Big 4" TIVAS			
DEPT OF ED/FEDLOAN SERVICING (PHEAA)	Non-Profit	800-699-2908	www.myfedloan.org
DEPT OF ED/GREAT LAKES	Non-Profit	800-236-4300	www.mygreatlakes.org
DEPT OF ED/NAVIENT	For Profit	800-722-1300	www.navient.com
DEPT OF ED/NELNET	For Profit	888-486-4722	www.nelnet.com
Five newly added Not-for-Profits (NFP's)			
DEPT OF ED/CORNERSTONE (UHEAA)	Non-Profit	800-663-1662	www.mycornerstoneloan.org
DEPT OF ED/HESC–EDFINANCIAL	Non-Profit	855-337-6884	www.edfinancial.com
DEPT OF ED/GRANITE STATE–GSMR–NH	Non-Profit	888-556-0022	www.gsmr.org
DEPT OF ED/MOHELA	Non-Profit	888-866-4352	www.mohela.com
DEPT OF ED/OSLA SERVICING	Non-Profit	866-264-9762	www.osla.org

Source: Studentaid.ed.gov

If you are unsure who services your federal student loan, simply access the National Student Loan Data System (NSLDS) website at: http://*www.nslds.ed.gov*. This is a centralized Department of Education website that lists every federal student loan that has been issued in your name along with its assigned servicer. First, you will have to create a Federal Student Aid identification number (FSA ID) to gain access.

How are the federal loan servicers compensated?
The Department of Education pays the federal loan servicers a fee to administer its own Federal Direct Loan Program (FDLP) loans and also a growing portfolio of older Federal Family Education Loan (FFEL) Program loans it continues to acquire from bank and financial institutions that wish to exit the student loan business. The Department of Education compensates the current list of federal loan servicers based on a formula that provides a higher payout according to a loan's status.

(In order from the highest payout terms to the lowest payout terms):
Borrower loans are in repayment status and are current (i.e., not delinquent).
Borrower loans are in repayment status but are delinquent.
Borrower loans are in repayment status and are current, but the borrower loans are in an elected period of qualified deferment (other than in-school or grace period), or forbearance.
Borrower loans are in an in-school or grace period deferment status.[14]

How are the federal loan servicers measured for performance?
30 percent—the percentage of borrowers in current status
15 percent—the percentage of borrowers over ninety days delinquent
15 percent—the percentage of borrowers in default
35 percent—borrower satisfaction survey results
5 percent—federal employee satisfaction survey results[15]

CHAPTER 2

Traditional Repayment Plans

It is incumbent on every generation to pay its own debts as it goes. A principle which if acted on would save one-half the wars of the world.

—Thomas Jefferson

Oh, the fretful arrival of the first student loan installment bill … "I can't afford this!"

Current Balance: $11,275.00

Your Payment Due: *$123.76*

Or … "This bill is more than I pay for my car note!"

Current Balance: $32,500.00

Your Payment Due: *$356.75*

Or worse yet … "This bill is more money than my monthly mortgage payment!"

Current Balance: $296,577.00

Your Payment Due: *$3,255.50*

Granted these first bills can seem-like a huge sum. But they are also meant to nudge the majority in a preferred direction that benefits the future growth and solvency of the government's Direct Loan Program. Under current congressional guidelines, your federal loan servicer is *required* to initially bill *all* borrowers based on a standard ten-year repayment plan.

Why so?
It's Banking 101. The government has to borrow money (ten-year treasury notes) in order to lend to you, and it has guaranteed its investors against its own default. The government hopes that you can closely match this same time period on payback and guarantee it against your own default. The greater the number of students who are able to do that, the greater the taxpayer risk is reduced. Currently, roughly 62 percent of all federal student loan borrowers choose to remain on the standard ten-year repayment plan.[16] The subtle nudge works!

The Standard Ten-Year (Fixed) Plan
As stated earlier, all federal loan borrowers will automatically be placed on this plan initially. Current and past congressional leaders have proposed a change to this policy, but for now, the standard ten-year plan is it. The standard ten-year schedule is the American classic of all student loan repayment plans. The payments remain fixed (level) for the entire life of the loan. It requires the highest monthly payment of any repayment plan option, and therefore, not everyone is fortunate enough to afford it. As a participating member of this exclusive club, you will send the silent message to your creditors that you are a responsible borrower. The major credit bureaus will adore you and will also reward you. And you will save the most in total interest payments versus alternative repayment plans.

The standard ten-year repayment schedule is also the simplest schedule to analyze. It requires a greater monthly payment so that a greater percentage of your hard-earned dollars are allocated to your principal balance than with alternative repayment schedules. This occurs from your first monthly payment to your final payment—the 120th month. Simple, yes, but the underlying financial concept is still often misunderstood. A four-year college graduate once expressed her dissatisfaction because it appeared to her that "I am paying about a fifty percent interest rate on my federal student loan! What can I do about this?" she asked bluntly. Was she really paying a 50 percent rate of interest on her loan? Of course not. But don't giggle either. She had actually taken the time to analyze her statement a bit. In the process, she had made an important conceptual discovery about the standard ten-year repayment schedule. Let's examine her discovery more closely.

Example:
Direct Loan Unsubsidized (DLUNST)
Loan balance: $5,872.00
Loan interest rate: 6.8%
Term (in years): 10
Fixed monthly installment: $67.58

Note: It doesn't matter what loan amount you use, $30,000 or $750,000, for example. Any loan amount will display the same percentage allocation as below, given this fixed interest rate, term and a simple twelve month, 360-day year amortization schedule.

This $67.58 fixed monthly payment gets allocated as follows:

Month	Principal	% Payment Principal	Interest	% Payment Interest	Payoff
		Key Concept!		Key Concept!	
1	$34.30	50.76%	$33.27	49.24%	$5,837.70
2	$34.49	51.05%	$33.08	48.95%	$5,803.20
3	$34.69	51.34%	$32.88	48.66%	$5,768.51
4	$34.89	51.63%	$32.69	48.37%	$5,733.63
5	$35.08	51.92%	$32.49	48.08%	$5,698.54
6	$35.28	52.21%	$32.29	47.79%	$5,663.26
7	$35.48	52.51%	$32.09	47.49%	$5,627.78
8	$35.68	52.81%	$31.89	47.19%	$5,592.09
9	$35.89	53.11%	$31.69	46.89%	$5,556.20
10	$36.09	53.41%	$31.49	46.59%	$5,520.11
11	$36.29	53.71%	$31.28	46.29%	$5,483.82
12	$36.50	54.01%	$31.07	45.99%	$5,447.32
24	$39.06	57.80%	$28.51	42.20%	$4,992.84
36	$41.80	61.86%	$25.77	38.14%	$4,506.48
48	$44.73	66.20%	$22.84	33.80%	$3,986.00
60	$47.87	70.84%	$19.70	29.16%	$3,429.00
72	$51.23	75.81%	$16.34	24.19%	$2,832.92
84	$54.83	81.13%	$12.75	18.87%	$2,195.02
96	$58.67	86.83%	$8.90	13.17%	$1,512.36
108	$62.79	92.92%	$4.79	7.08%	$781.81
120	$67.19	99.44%	$0.38	0.56%	$0.00

From your very first payment, a greater amount or 50.7 percent (50.7 cents out of every dollar) is allocated to principal under this standard ten-year repayment schedule example. With each successive monthly payment, the percentage allocation to principal will gradually increase, ending at 99 percent on the very last payment in the 120th month. This higher payment allocation to principal from the first payment to the last payment is the main difference between the ten-year repayment schedule and other repayment plans. This is why you will pay the least amount of interest with this plan option than with any other repayment choice. Perhaps the good fortune your new job brings will allow you to participate in this plan. Even with good fortune, however, it is paramount that you practice discipline and make the necessary adjustments to your spending habits and other daily lifestyle choices to stay the course and consistently satisfy these higher, scheduled monthly payments. It will take tremendous sacrifice. For others, the higher payments simply are not doable.

The Interest Rate Does Matter!
The 6.8 percent fixed interest rate in the above example was chosen for a good reason. At that rate of interest, the percentage allocation of your first installment payment to principal is less than one percentage point greater than the percentage allocated to interest (6.9 percent is the break-even point). This 6.8 percent interest rate had been the rate charged many undergraduate borrowers on their student loans during the school years 2006 through 2011. Coincidental on the part of Congress? You decide. Some may argue that this 6.8 percent fixed interest rate was set artificially too high and for much too long a period of time, given the weak economic conditions of the period. The laws of economics dictate that if the interest cost to borrow new funds is set too high, demand will dissipate. So, if Congress didn't act to lower its student loan borrower rates, as it did in 2013, many students may have become dispirited about pursuing higher education. Not exactly the preferred outcome for a Democratic administration that wishes to expand ever higher the education participation rates in America through its Federal Direct Loan Program.

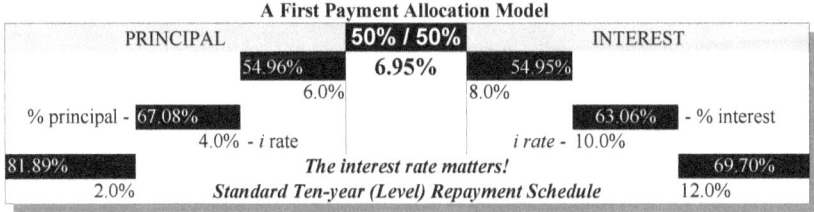

Regardless of the loan balance (assuming a thirty day payment cycle and a twelve month, 360 day amortization).

Two Reasons Your Actual Payment Allocation May Differ from the Above

First, the above chart is based on a consistent thirty-day month, 360-day year. Of course, your loan interest accrual will be based on a 365-day year with some months containing more days than others (and a leap year). Second, your payments may get credited on different days from month to month depending on whether your due date falls on a weekend or on a holiday, and therefore, your exact payment allocation may differ slightly from month to month. The purpose of this chapter is to capture the illustration that is otherwise lost as a result of these minor variations.

Eligible Federal Loans

Federal Direct Loan Program (FDLP) loans—issued from 2002 and beyond:

- Direct Loan Subsidized Stafford (DLSTFD)
- Direct Loan Unsubsidized Stafford (DLUNST)
- Direct PLUS loan issued to a graduate student or professional (DLPLGB)
- Direct PLUS loan issued to a parent for the benefit of a dependent student (DLPLUS)
- Direct Subsidized Consolidation (DLSCNS)
- Direct Unsubsidized Consolidation (DLUNCS)

Federal Family Education Loan (FFEL)—These loans may have been issued prior to 2008:

- FFEL Subsidized Stafford (STFD)
- FFEL Unsubsidized Stafford (UNSTFD)
- FFEL Graduate PLUS (PLUSGB)

- FFEL Parent PLUS (PLUS)
- FFEL Subsidized Consolidation (SUBCNS)
- FFEL Unsubsidized Consolidation (UNCNS)

Eligible Balance Requirements
All federal loan balances qualify (if you can afford it!).[17]

Other Traditional Repayment Plan Options
If the required monthly installment amount under a standard ten-year level repayment schedule is deemed unaffordable, the following chart will guide you to other responsible repayment options that may serve as good substitutes.

Presented in order from the least to the most in total interest payments over time:

Traditional Repayment Plan Selection Hierarchy

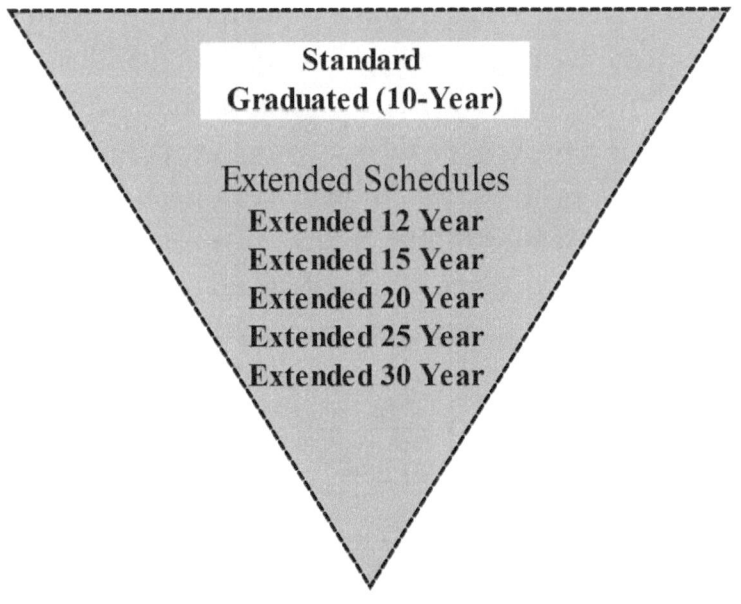

The menu of alternative yet still traditional repayment schedule offerings may *vary* among federal loan servicers. I suggest you call your assigned loan servicer to inquire. However, a full menu of repayment plan options is available to borrowers (dependent on your total outstanding loan balance and loan type) through the process of loan consolidation. (More on this topic in chapter 8.)

The Graduated Ten-Year Plan

The ten-year graduated repayment schedule offers a lower initial payment than its counterpart (the ten-year level repayment plan). Two caveats exist with these lower initial payments, however. First, a lower initial payment means less principal erosion in the early years of repayment (i.e., years one through five). Since a fixed rate of interest is charged on this higher principal balance over a longer period of time, you will pay more interest than that amount paid under a standard level ten-year payment plan. Second, your monthly installment will increase every two years (twenty-four months). Upon completion of this initial twenty-four month period, your monthly installment will then increase a minimum of four additional times (at the beginning of year three, again in year five, year seven, and year nine) over a ten-year payment period. Many borrowers are often caught off guard by these scheduled payment increases. Either they forget over time, or they have already budgeted elsewhere and find it difficult to juggle these higher payments as they occur. Lastly, to satisfy your entire outstanding balance in ten years, your final payment must closely approximate (but not exceed) three times the initial payment amount.[18]

TRADITIONAL REPAYMENT PLANS

Example:
Direct Loan Unsubsidized (DLUNST)
Loan balance: $5,872.00
Loan interest rate: 6.8%
Term (in years): 10

Your payment from months one to twenty-four will remain level at $38.56.
The first payment-reset period will occur between months twenty-five through forty-eight. The required fixed payments will increase to $53.53 per month.
The second payment-reset period will occur between months forty-nine through seventy-two. The required fixed payments will increase to $71.09 per month.
The third payment-reset period will occur between months seventy-three through ninety-six. The required fixed payments will increase to $91.22 per month.
The fourth and final increase period will occur between months ninety-seven through 120. The final fixed payments will increase to $106.91 to satisfy the loan in full in ten years.

	Month	Payment	Principal	Key Concept! % Payment Principal	Interest	Key Concept! % Payment Interest	Payoff
Payments 1-24	1	$38.56	$5.28	*13.70%*	$33.27	*86.30%*	$5,866.72
	24	$38.56	$6.01	*15.60%*	$32.54	*84.40%*	$5,736.62
Payments 25-48	25	$53.53	$21.02	*39.27%*	$32.51	*60.73%*	$5,715.60
	48	$53.53	$23.94	*44.72%*	$29.59	*55.28%*	$5,197.89
Payments 49-72	49	$71.09	$41.64	*58.57%*	$29.45	*41.43%*	$5,156.26
	72	$71.09	$47.41	*66.70%*	$23.68	*33.30%*	$4,130.73
Payments 73-96	73	$91.22	$67.81	*74.34%*	$23.41	*25.66%*	$4,062.92
	96	$91.22	$77.22	*84.66%*	$14.00	*15.34%*	$2,392.73
Payments 97-120	97	$106.91	$93.35	*87.32%*	$13.56	*12.68%*	$2,299.38
	120	$106.91	$106.31	*99.44%*	$0.60	*0.56%*	$0.00

Note: Each loan servicer's formula to determine your monthly payment schedule may vary. The federal guidelines require that, at a minimum, your first monthly payment must be sufficient enough to have at least one dollar of principal satisfied.[19] The above example uses a four-dollar minimum in the first month. I suggest you call your federal loan servicer.

Eligible Federal Loans
Federal Direct Loan Program (FDLP) loans—issued from 2002 and beyond:

- Direct Loan Subsidized Stafford (DLSTFD)
- Direct Loan Unsubsidized Stafford (DLUNST)
- Direct PLUS loan issued to a graduate student or professional (DLPLGB)
- Direct PLUS loan issued to a parent for the benefit of a dependent student (DLPLUS)
- Direct Loan Subsidized Consolidation (DLSCNS)
- Direct Loan Unsubsidized Consolidation (DLUNCS)

Federal Family Education Loan (FFEL)—These loans may have been issued prior to 2008:

- FFEL Subsidized Stafford (STFD)
- FFEL Unsubsidized Stafford (UNSTFD)
- FFEL Graduate PLUS (PLUSGB)
- FFEL Parent PLUS (PLUS)
- FFEL Subsidized Consolidation (SUBCNS)
- FFEL Unsubsidized Consolidation (UNCNS)[20]

Eligible Balance Requirements
Not all loan balances qualify. You must have at least forty-eight months of term (four years) remaining to qualify.[21]

Extended-Year Repayment Schedules
Not every borrower is eligible to participate in traditional extended-year repayment plans. These plans require minimum balances to participate as follows:

Minimum Loan Balance Eligibility Requirements

Minimum Loan Balance Requirements

>$7,500.00 - $10,000.00 - 12 year Extended Schedule
>$10,000.00 - $20,000.00 - 15 year
>$20,000.00 - $40,000.00 - 20 years
>$40,000.00 - $60,000.00 - 25 years
>$60,000.00 - 30 years

Eligible Federal Loans
Federal Direct Loan Program (FDLP) loans—issued from 2002 and beyond:

- Direct Loan Subsidized Stafford (DLSTFD)
- Direct Loan Unsubsidized Stafford (DLUNST)
- Direct PLUS loan issued to a graduate student or professional (DLPLGB)
- Direct PLUS loan issued to a parent for the benefit of a dependent student (DLPLUS)
- Direct Loan Subsidized Consolidation (DLSCNS)
- Direct Loan Unsubsidized Consolidation (DLUNCS)

Federal Family Education Loan (FFEL)—These loans may have been issued prior to 2008:

- FFEL Subsidized Stafford (STFD)
- FFEL Unsubsidized Stafford (UNSTFD)
- FFEL Graduate PLUS (PLUSGB)
- FFEL Parent PLUS (PLUS)
- FFEL Subsidized Consolidation (SUBCNS)
- FFEL Unsubsidized Consolidation (UNCNS)

Note: Not all federal loan servicers offer the same repayment schedules. Check with your assigned federal loan servicer for individual servicer repayment plan offerings.

The Extended Twenty-Five-Year Fixed Plan

To participate in the twenty-five-year extended fixed repayment schedule you must meet some additional criteria.

1. Your total balance of *either* outstanding direct loans *or* outstanding FFEL Program loans must be equal to or greater than $30,000.
   and
2. You must have been a new borrower as of October 7, 1998, or later.[22]

Examples:

Borrower 1:
Total outstanding loans balance is $47,500, no loans outstanding prior to October 7, 1998. Total balance of direct loans equals $32,500. Total balance of FFEL loans equals $15,000. This borrower *qualifies*. The direct loan balance exceeds $30,000, so *all* loans may participate—even the FFEL loans!

Borrower 2:
Total outstanding loans balance is $32,100, no loans outstanding prior to October 7, 1998. Total balance of direct loans equals $28,500. Total balance of FFEL loans equals $3,600.
This borrower *does not qualify!* Neither the direct loan balances (calculated as a separate total) nor the FFEL loan balances (calculated as a separate total) exceed the $30,000 threshold. Yes, combined they do, but this does not count.

Example:

Total balance of six separate direct loans: $31,000
Loan interest rate: 6.8%
Term (in years): 25
Note: It doesn't matter what loan amount you use, $30,000 or $750,000, for example. Any loan amount will display the same percentage allocation as below, given this fixed interest rate, term and a simple twelve month, 360-day year amortization schedule.

Month	% Payment Principal *Key Concept!*	% Payment Interest *Key Concept!*	Payoff
1	*18.36%*	*81.64%*	$30,960.50
24	*20.90%*	*79.10%*	$29,987.69
36	*22.37%*	*77.63%*	$29,427.66
48	*23.94%*	*76.06%*	$28,828.34
60	*25.62%*	*74.38%*	$28,186.98
72	*27.42%*	*72.58%*	$27,500.62
84	*29.34%*	*70.66%*	$26,766.10
96	*31.40%*	*68.60%*	$25,980.04
108	*33.60%*	*66.40%*	$25,138.84
120	*35.96%*	*64.04%*	$24,238.62
132	*38.48%*	*61.52%*	$23,275.24
144	*41.18%*	*58.82%*	$22,244.27
156	*44.07%*	*55.93%*	$21,140.97
168	*47.16%*	*52.84%*	$19,960.26
180	*50.47%*	*49.53%*	$18,696.71
192	*54.01%*	*45.99%*	$17,344.51
204	*57.80%*	*42.20%*	$15,897.44
216	*61.86%*	*38.14%*	$14,348.84
228	*66.20%*	*33.80%*	$12,691.60
240	*70.84%*	*29.16%*	$10,918.08
252	*75.81%*	*24.19%*	$9,020.13
264	*81.13%*	*18.87%*	$6,989.03
276	*86.83%*	*13.17%*	$4,815.42
288	*92.92%*	*7.08%*	$2,489.31
300	*99.44%*	*0.56%*	$0.00

Eligible Loans

Federal Direct Loan Program (FDLP) loans—issued from 2002 and beyond:

- Direct Loan Subsidized Stafford (DLSTFD)
- Direct Loan Unsubsidized Stafford (DLUNST)
- Direct PLUS loan issued to a graduate student or professional (DLPLGB)
- Direct PLUS loan issued to a parent for the benefit of a dependent student (DLPLUS)
- Direct Loan Subsidized Consolidation (DLSCNS)
- Direct Loan Unsubsidized Consolidation (DLUNCS)

Federal Family Education Loan (FFEL)—These loans may have been issued prior to 2008:

- FFEL Subsidized Stafford (STFD)
- FFEL Unsubsidized Stafford (UNSTFD)
- FFEL Graduate PLUS (PLUSGB)
- FFEL Parent PLUS (PLUS)
- FFEL Subsidized Consolidation (SUBCNS)
- FFEL Unsubsidized Consolidation (UNCNS)

The Extended Twenty-Five-Year Graduated Plan

The same rules apply here as with the twenty-five-year fixed plan. Using the same loan balance and interest rate as in the above twenty-five-year fixed repayment example yields:

	Month	Payment	Principal	% Payment Principal	Interest	% Payment Interest	Payoff
				Key Concept!		Key Concept!	
Payments 1-24	1	$404.53	$4.00	0.99%	$400.53	99.01%	$69,906.66
	24	$404.53	$4.57	1.13%	$399.97	98.87%	$69,807.95
Payments 25-48	25	$422.62	$22.68	5.37%	$399.94	94.63%	$69,785.27
	48	$422.62	$25.86	6.12%	$396.76	93.88%	$69,226.33
Payments 49-72	49	$441.51	$44.90	10.17%	$396.61	89.83%	$69,181.43
	72	$441.51	$51.20	11.60%	$390.30	88.40%	$68,074.69
Payments 73-96	73	$461.24	$71.23	15.44%	$390.01	84.56%	$68,003.46
	96	$461.24	$81.23	17.61%	$380.01	82.39%	$66,247.62
Payments 97-120	97	$481.86	$102.32	21.23%	$379.54	78.77%	$66,145.30
	120	$481.86	$116.68	24.22%	$365.18	75.78%	$63,623.21
Payments 121-144	121	$503.40	$138.89	27.59%	$364.51	72.41%	$63,484.32
	144	$503.40	$158.39	31.47%	$345.01	68.53%	$60,060.67
Payments 145-168	145	$525.90	$181.80	34.57%	$344.10	65.43%	$59,878.86
	168	$525.90	$207.33	39.42%	$318.57	60.58%	$55,397.44
Payments 169-192	169	$549.41	$232.03	42.23%	$317.38	57.77%	$55,165.41
	192	$549.41	$264.61	48.16%	$284.80	51.84%	$49,445.97
Payments 193-216	193	$573.97	$290.68	50.64%	$283.28	49.36%	$49,155.28
	216	$573.97	$331.50	57.76%	$242.47	42.24%	$41,990.00
Payments 217-240	217	$599.62	$359.06	59.88%	$240.57	40.12%	$41,630.94
	240	$599.62	$409.48	68.29%	$190.15	31.71%	$32,780.28
Payments 241-264	241	$626.43	$438.62	70.02%	$187.80	29.98%	$32,341.66
	264	$626.43	$500.21	79.85%	$126.21	20.15%	$21,529.69
Payments 265-288	265	$654.43	$531.08	81.15%	$123.35	18.85%	$20,998.60
	288	$654.43	$605.66	92.55%	$48.77	7.45%	$7,907.57
Payments 289-300	289	$683.76	$638.46	93.37%	$45.30	6.63%	$7,269.12
	300	$683.76	$679.87	99.43%	$3.90	0.57%	$0.00

Note: Not all federal loan servicers offer the same extended-term repayment schedules. Check with your assigned servicer for individual servicer repayment plan offerings.

CHAPTER 3

Income-Driven Repayment—The Rage!

> 'Tis against some men's principle to pay interest, and seems against others interest to pay the principal.
> —Benjamin Franklin

This is how borrowers in the previous chapter turned their large installment bill:

From:

Current Balance: $11,275.00

| Your Payment Due: | $123.76 |

To:

Current Balance: $11,275.00

| Your Payment Due: | $0.00 |

From:

Current Balance: $32,500.00

| Your Payment Due: | $356.75 |

To:

Current Balance: $32,500.00

| Your Payment Due: | $86.23 |

From:

Current Balance: $296,577.00

| Your Payment Due: | $3,255.50 |

To:

Current Balance: $296,577.00

| Your Payment Due: | $852.90 |

The September 2007 passage of the College Cost Reduction and Access Act expanded student loan repayment schedules known as income-driven repayment plans. This legislation marks a dramatic shift in the American attitude toward the borrower's responsibility for student loan debt repayment obligations.[23]

An income-driven plan is exactly as the name implies: a repayment schedule predicated on one's adjusted gross income and family size (with caveats, of course). These plans offer US student loan borrowers repayment choices modeled after those in Europe and Australia, whereby our government limits the borrower's payment obligation from 10 to 20 percent of discretionary income and leaves open-ended the total amount of loan balance forgiveness at a set end point ... twenty or twenty-five years.

The Benefits

Income-driven repayment schedules may offer you the lowest monthly payment (as low as a $0.00 monthly installment) when compared to other traditional repayment schedules (presented in chapter 2). These income-driven repayment schedules also may better match your required monthly installments to your immediate financial situation. The word you will hear uttered most with these plans is *forgiveness*. Before you get too excited, remember this is Marketing 101. And yes, the government markets its program benefits just as a Fortune 500 company markets its products. In government speak, the word *forgiveness* leads one to conjure up the purest interpretation of the word. Don't be fooled! The Department of Education will only forgive a portion of your total liability, not 100 percent. You will incur a tax on the amount forgiven at your then/current personal income tax rate. Then you'll owe the IRS!

The Different Types of Income-Driven Repayment Schedules

There are currently four types of income-driven plans:

- Pay As You Earn (PAYE)
- Revised Pay As You Earn (REPAYE), available as of December 16, 2015
- Income-Based Repayment (IBR)
- Income-Contingent Repayment (ICR)

Note: New borrowers who apply for IBR will receive a reduced payment requirement limited to only 10 percent of discretionary income and partial loan forgiveness after only twenty years (240 qualified monthly payments). To qualify for this new borrower classification under IBR, you must be considered a new direct loan borrower as of July 1, 2014 with no prior outstanding loan balance on a FDLP or FFEL Program loan when you received a direct loan on or after July 1, 2014).[24] All other plan features associated with IBR still apply. Therefore, in my opinion, IBR, even for those who qualify under the new borrower classification, is inferior to Pay As You Earn repayment.

Which income-driven repayment plans attract the most in borrower dollars?

With just a brief glance at the chart below, you can quickly identify the repayment plans that have attracted the largest amount of money (in billions of dollars) as of Q3 (third quarter) 2016:

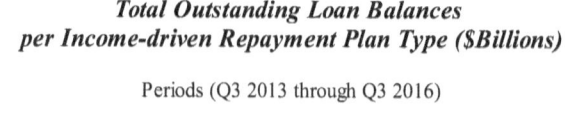

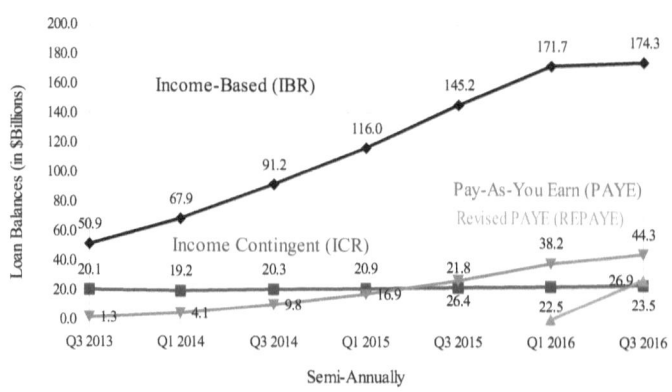

Source: Department of Education

Observe the immediate spike in new dollar flows into the Revised Pay As You Earn (REPAYE) repayment plan and the subsequent leveling-off of money that continues to flow into the Income-Based Repayment schedule. The chart pattern is not coincidental. Borrowers begin to swap the Income-Based Repayment plan for the Revised Pay As You Earn repayment plan. It is this simple!

Which income-driven repayment plans attract the largest number of participants?
Approximately 5.27 million individuals, or 24.8 percent of all individuals who now repay on Federal Direct Loan Portfolio loans, choose to participate in income-driven repayment plans (calculated results from raw data findings in the Department of Education Direct Loan Portfolio Q3 [third quarter] 2016 report). On the same note, the total number of individuals who participate in income-driven repayment plans has risen by a stellar 49.41 percent average annual rate from Q3 2013 to Q3 2016.

However, not all income-driven repayment plans are equal, when studied further based on their speed of rise in popularity. Revised Pay As You Earn is the fastest growing of the four income-driven repayment plans as of Q3 2016. Revised Pay As You Earn repayment appeals to a wider group of qualified borrowers across a larger span of age categories. Since its debut in late 2015, a total of .57 million individuals now participate in this repayment plan. Pay As You Earn has the second fastest participant growth rate but over a much longer period of study from Q3 2013 to Q3 2016. Participation has grown by a sustained and stellar 28.1 percent average rate per quarter. Total participants now number 1.0 million. Income-Based Repayment participation has also grown by an equally impressive average quarterly rate of 9.89 percent over this same three year time period. Participating borrowers now number an outsized 3.1 million. However, as a result of the recent introduction of the Revised Pay As You Earn repayment plan, any further participation rate increases for Income-Based Repayment appear highly unlikely. Income-Contingent Repayment—the oldest plan choice—declined by an average of -1.6 percent over this same three year period. Total participants now number .60 million borrowers.

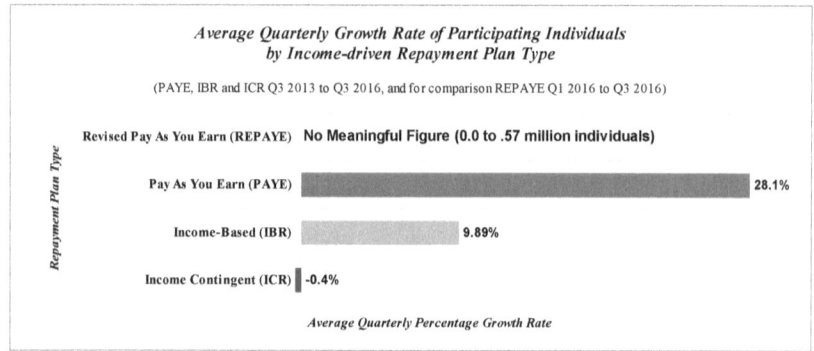

Source: Department of Education

A Further Explanation for the Growth

A primary reason why the Pay As You Earn repayment plan has experienced sustained participation growth among qualified, often younger, less established borrowers is simple. Many are strapped with huge amounts of student loan debt soon after graduation. They struggle to find stability both financially and professionally amidst a weak economy and a stagnant job market. Pay As You Earn repayment offers these qualified borrowers a lower payment as a percentage of total income. An added lure is the Congressional promise of partial loan forgiveness in the shortest length of time – 20 years (240 qualified payments).

Revised Pay As You Earn participation has likely risen for the same reasons among middle-aged borrowers. They too struggle financially as they juggle money to support a family, a mortgage and to service lingering, high balance student loan debt. These same borrowers prove more than eager to switch to any repayment plan that offers them even the slightest payment reduction or a quicker path to partial loan forgiveness. Their unsurprising strategy: swap debt from Income-Based Repayment to the Revised Pay As You Earn repayment plan.

A professional college graduate once posed this question: "I have well over one hundred thousand dollars in student loan debt. I'd like to get engaged, but I am afraid that my girlfriend will struggle to say 'yes' in worry that she'll have to help pay for my student loans. My question to you is … Can I get married and keep my installment payment the same as it is now, based only on my income, so my girlfriend doesn't feel responsible to help pay back my student loans?" [Response] Yes.
"Awesome! I'll be engaged by tonight!"

Do I qualify for an income-driven repayment (IDR) plan?
It depends on a combination of factors, mainly:

- Tax filing status (based on the previous year's tax filings)
- Income level (adjusted gross income (AGI) from the previous year's tax filing, or current pay gross earnings before taxes and other pretax deductions).
- Family size (For student loan purposes, this figure may differ from the number of dependents claimed for tax purposes.)[25]

To qualify for either Pay As You Earn or Income-Based Repayment, you must also meet this additional criteria: You must have a partial financial hardship (PFH) in the year that you apply. If, in a later year, it is determined that you no longer have a partial financial hardship based on your then current level of taxable income and family size, you may continue to participate in the plan.

Note: Revised Pay As You Earn (REPAYE) and Income-Contingent Repayment (ICR) do not require a partial financial hardship. All income levels qualify.

How is discretionary income determined?
To determine one's *discretionary income*, we rely on the Department of Health and Human Services (HHS) poverty guideline release each year in mid-January (as presented in chapter 1). First, we must adjust these baseline poverty guideline figures by a multiplication factor of 150 percent.[23] Second, we calculate discretionary income. Discretionary income is determined by the difference between the *lesser* of one's gross income—either the previous tax year's adjusted gross income (AGI) divided by twelve months, or one's current gross earnings before taxes and other pretax deductions.[24]

How is a partial Financial hardship (PFH) measured?
A partial financial hardship exists if the computed installment under either Pay As You Earn at 10 percent of your discretionary income, or Income-Based Repayment at 15 percent of discretionary income (10 percent for new borrowers), is *less than* the required payment under a standard ten-year fixed repayment schedule scenario. Here is an example:

Recall Sam, our recent college graduate from chapter 1. Suppose Sam resides in Ohio and is single. Sam did file taxes last year as a college student, but his current income has since increased significantly. His current pay stubs are his only income documentation. His gross monthly earnings are $2,110.33.

Let's consider this simplified version of Sam's loan portfolio

Loan Type	Disbursement	Original Bal.	Current Bal.	*i* Rate	Outstanding *i*	Payoff
DLUNST	08/15/2014	$2,000.00	$2,114.25	4.66%	$0.00	$2,114.25
DLSTFD	08/15/2014	$5,500.00	$5,500.00	4.66%	$0.00	$5,500.00
DLUNST	08/18/2013	$2,000.00	$2,172.20	3.86%	$0.00	$2,172.20
DLSTFD	08/18/2013	$5,500.00	$5,606.72	3.86%	$0.00	$5,606.72
DLUNST	08/20/2012	$2,000.00	$2,438.45	6.80%	$0.00	$2,438.45
DLSTFD	08/20/2012	$4,500.00	$4,575.44	3.40%	$0.00	$4,575.44
DLUNST	08/15/2011	$2,000.00	$2,575.35	6.80%	$0.00	$2,575.35
DLSTFD	08/15/2011	$3,500.00	$3,500.00	3.40%	$0.00	$3,500.00
Total		$27,000.00	$28,482.41		$0.00	$28,482.41

We now have the necessary data to determine whether or not Sam has a PFH and which income-driven repayment plan offers him the best option.

Step 1: Locate Sam's poverty guideline figure from the 2015 Federal Poverty Guidelines. Adjusted by a factor of 150 percent and divided by 12 months, that amount equals $1,471.25.

Note: Recognize that the current balance figure for Sam's portfolio above has increased to $28,482.41 (see chapter 1, pp. 2-4). We assume that Sam, like most recent college graduates, simply could not afford to satisfy any portion of the $1,482.41 interest notice he received with a December 20 due date. As a result, $1,482.41 in interest has capitalized. Sam's $0.00 outstanding interest balance figure assumes that Sam has paid, not only the $115.56 of interest that accrued between November 16 and December 20 (see chapter 1, p. 5), but also that he has paid any additional interest accrued to date. Sam now patiently awaits his loan servicer decision of approval on an income-driven repayment (IDR) schedule application.

2015 POVERTY GUIDELINES FOR THE 48 CONTIGUOUS STATES & D.C.

Family Size	Annual Poverty Guidelines	150% of Annual Poverty Guideline	Monthly
1	$11,770	$17,655	$1,471.25
2	15,930	23,895	1,991.25
3	20,090	30,135	2,511.25
4	24,250	36,375	3,031.25
5	28,410	42,615	3,551.25
6	32,570	48,855	4,071.25
7	36,730	55,095	4,591.25
8	40,890	61,335	5,111.25

For families/households with more than 8 persons, add $4,160 for each additional person.

2015 POVERTY GUIDELINES FOR ALASKA

Family Size	Annual Poverty Guidelines	150% of Annual Poverty Guideline	Monthly
1	$14,720	$22,080	$1,840.00
2	19,920	29,880	2,490.00
3	25,120	37,680	3,140.00
4	30,320	45,480	3,790.00
5	35,520	53,280	4,440.00
6	40,720	61,080	5,090.00
7	45,920	68,880	5,740.00
8	51,120	76,680	6,390.00

For families/households with more than 8 persons, add $5,200 for each additional person.

2015 POVERTY GUIDELINES FOR HAWAII

Family Size	Annual Poverty Guidelines	150% of Annual Poverty Guideline	Monthly
1	$13,550	$20,325	$1,693.75
2	18,330	27,495	2,291.25
3	23,110	34,665	2,888.75
4	27,890	41,835	3,486.25
5	32,670	49,005	4,083.75
6	37,450	56,175	4,681.25
7	42,230	63,345	5,278.75
8	47,010	70,515	5,876.25

For families/households with more than 8 persons, add $4,780 for each additional person.
Source: hhs.gov

Step 2: Calculate the difference between Sam's monthly gross earnings (before taxes) and his poverty guideline allowance in step one.

$2,110.33 - $1,471.25 = $639.08.

Step 3: Calculate Sam's required monthly payment under a standard ten-year fixed repayment schedule according to the formula below or in Excel.

Note: If you calculate the total portfolio value by its weighted average interest rate (chapter 8), the answer will differ slightly from the more precise one derived by calculating each loan separately.

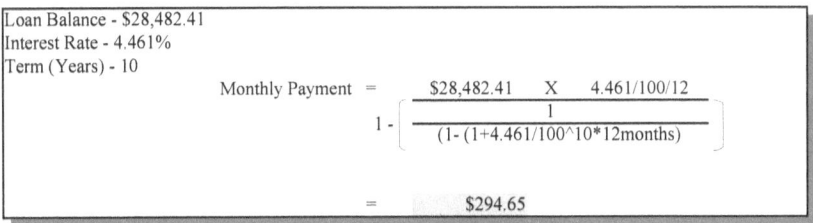

In Excel you may calculate the above as follows:

	Column A	B
Row 2	Current Balance	$28,482.41
3	Rate	4.461
4	Term (Yrs)	10
5	Payment (Monthly)	=$B$2*($B$3/100/12)/(1-(1/(1+$B$3/100/12)^($B$4*12)))

The more precise result is:

Loan Type	Disbursement	Current Bal.	Payoff Bal.	Rate	Term (in Years)	Installment
DLUNST	08/15/14	$2,114.25	$2,114.25	4.66%	10	$22.08
DLSTFD	08/15/14	$5,500.00	$5,500.00	4.66%	10	$57.43
DLUNST	08/18/13	$2,172.20	$2,172.20	3.86%	10	$21.85
DLSTFD	08/18/13	$5,606.72	$5,606.72	3.86%	10	$56.39
DLUNST	08/20/12	$2,438.45	$2,438.45	6.80%	10	$28.06
DLSTFD	08/20/12	$4,575.44	$4,575.44	3.40%	10	$45.03
DLUNST	08/15/11	$2,575.35	$2,575.35	6.80%	10	$29.64
DLSTFD	08/15/11	$3,500.00	$3,500.00	3.40%	10	$34.45
Total		$28,482.41	$28,482.41			$294.93

Based on the above, Sam's PFH of his calculated monthly payment is less than $294.93 under both the Pay As You Earn repayment schedule and the Income-Based Repayment schedule. Now all that remains is to look at each repayment schedule independently to determine in which plan Sam qualifies to participate.

Pay As You Earn, a Third-Generation Repayment Plan

Pay As You Earn reduces your monthly installment to 10 percent of discretionary income. This repayment schedule offers borrowers with a remaining balance partial loan forgiveness after twenty years (240 qualified payments).[25]

How does Sam's monthly installment calculate under the Pay As You Earn repayment plan?

Pay-As-You Earn (PAYE) Repayment Plan

Loan Type	Disbursement	% Weight	Installment	Accrued i	Subsidy	Outstanding i	Payoff Bal.
DLUNST	08/15/14	7.42%	$4.74	$8.10		$3.35	$2,117.60
DLSTFD	08/15/14	19.31%	$12.34	$21.07	$8.73	$0.00	$5,500.00
DLUNST	08/18/13	7.63%	$4.87	$6.89		$2.02	$2,174.22
DLSTFD	08/18/13	19.68%	$12.58	$17.79	$5.21	$0.00	$5,606.72
DLUNST	08/20/12	8.56%	$5.47	$13.63		$8.16	$2,446.61
DLSTFD	08/20/12	16.06%	$10.27	$12.79	$2.52	$0.00	$4,575.44
DLUNST	08/15/11	9.04%	$5.78	$14.39		$8.62	$2,583.97
DLSTFD	08/15/11	12.29%	$7.85	$9.78	$1.93	$0.00	$3,500.00
Total		100.00%	**$63.91**	**$104.43**	**$18.38**	**$22.14**	**$28,504.55**

(Assumes a 30 day month)

The Math Explained:
Sam's discretionary income is $2,110.33 - $1,471.25 = $639.08.

Sam's Pay As You Earn monthly installment equals $63.91 (10% x $639.08) or (.10 x $639.08).

The Key Takeaways:
√ The total monthly installment of $63.91 is allocated in payment to each individual loan in the portfolio by its percentage weight of the total portfolio (i.e., $4.74 = $63.91 x 7.42% where 7.42% = 2,114.25/$28,482.41).

√ The interest subsidy is only available to Pay As You Earn participants during years one through three. The interest subsidy per subsidized loan may range from 0 percent to 100 percent depending on the total required monthly installment (i.e., 47.49% = $8.73/$18.38).

√ Your credit score may be negatively impacted because of *negative amortization*. Negative amortization results when a monthly installment payment is too small to cover the monthly interest accrual on a loan and the loan balance moves in a negative direction (i.e., the loan balance increases rather than decreases).

Pay As You Earn Annual Recertification Requirement
You must formally submit your annual documentation to recertify your income and family size each year prior to the plan's anniversary date or a penalty will be assessed. Miss this deadline as a Pay As You Earn participant and the outstanding interest will capitalize as a form of penalty (but never more than 10 percent of the outstanding loan balance the day you entered Pay As You Earn). Future interest will then accrue daily based on this higher balance figure.[26] Yikes!

Pay As You Earn Eligibility Requirements

- Only Federal Direct Loan Program loans (FDLP) are eligible.
- You must have a partial financial hardship (PFH).
- You must have been a *new* borrower as of October 1, 2007 (or a repeat borrower with no prior outstanding loan

balances, i.e., previously paid in full), and you must have acquired a *new* direct loan on or after October 1, 2011.[27]

Pay As You Earn Eligible Loans
Federal Direct Loan Program (FDLP) loans (issued from 2002 and beyond):

- Direct Loan Subsidized Stafford (DLSTFD)
- Direct Loan Unsubsidized Stafford (DLUNST)
- Direct PLUS loan issued to a graduate student or professional (DLPLGB)
- Direct Loan Subsidized Consolidation (DLSCNS)
- Direct Loan Unsubsidized Consolidation (DLUNCS)

Note: A Direct PLUS loan issued to a parent for the benefit of a dependent student is ineligible, including any Direct Consolidation loan that contains a PLUS loan issued to a parent.

Income-Driven Repayment Plan Hierarchy

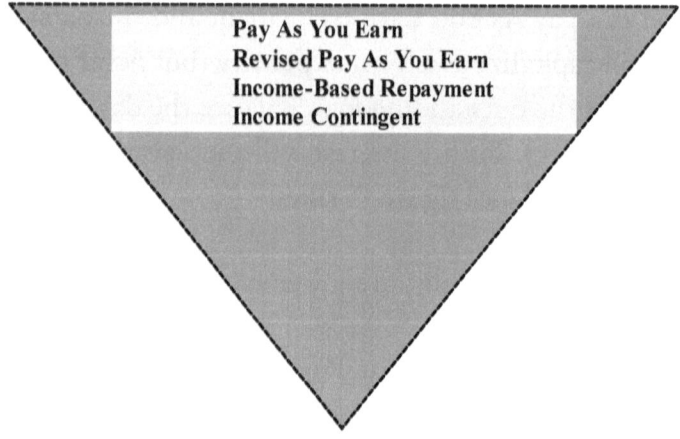

Revised Pay As You Earn Repayment Schedule
(as of December 16, 2015)

The Revised Pay As You Earn repayment schedule will mostly benefit a distinct, but smaller, segment of student loan borrowers, mainly graduate and professional students who have outstanding Direct PLUS loan for graduates or professionals (DLPLGB). Until now at least, this group of borrowers (i.e., physicians, dentists, lawyers, MBAs, teachers, scientists, etc.), who are most likely older in age and fall shy of the new borrower classification requirements under Pay As You Earn (those who still have student loan balances outstanding on loans disbursed prior to October 1, 2007, or no new loan disbursements after October 1, 2011), were limited to either traditional repayment plans or Income-Contingent Repayment. Not anymore. These highly educated borrowers may now qualify for much lower payments on normally higher loan balances. The addition of this repayment plan stays consistent with the federal government's goal to further mitigate the financial burden on borrowers.

The Revised Pay As You Earn repayment schedule may modestly lower payments for other middle-aged borrowers who were originally issued Federal Direct Loan Program (FDLP) loans in 2002 and beyond to pursue or obtain an undergraduate degree. For these borrowers, the Revised Pay As You Earn plan is nothing more than a congressional tinker—a modest payment reduction and a slightly shortened payment period. (See the schedule highlights below.)

A Summary of the Revised Pay As You Earn Repayment Schedule

- Only Federal Direct Loan Program (FDLP) loans qualify (similar to Income-Contingent Repayment).
- Eliminates the new borrower classification on direct loan disbursement dates (dissimilar to Pay As You Earn, which limits participation to only new borrowers with no loans outstanding prior to October 1, 2007, and at least one loan disbursed after October 1, 2011).
- No partial financial hardship (PFH) determination is required (similar to Income-Contingent Repayment).
- Payments are calculated at 10 percent of discretionary income (similar to Pay As You Earn).
- No capping of monthly payments. Your qualifying payment may exceed the standard fixed payment schedule (dissimilar to Pay As You Earn, which limits the monthly payment to no greater than the standard fixed payment).
- Partial loan forgiveness occurs in either twenty years (240 qualifying payments) on undergraduate level loans or twenty-five years (300 qualifying payments) on graduate or professional level loans.
- If you are married, *both* incomes are considered (dissimilar to Pay As You Earn, Income-Based Repayment, and Income-Contingent Repayment schedules that allow an exclusion of spousal income if a borrower has filed as married filing separately).
- Borrowers receive up to a 100 percent interest subsidy on any subsidized loans during the first three consecutive years of repayment (similar to Pay As You Earn and Income-Based Repayment). However, during subsequent

periods (after years one through three), the borrower is only responsible for *50 percent* of the residual (leftover) accrued interest on any subsidized loans after a qualified payment is met. For unsubsidized loans this 50 percent limit applies during all periods.

Note: Federal Direct PLUS loans issued to a parent for the benefit of a dependent student (DLPLUS) are *not* eligible to participate in Revised Pay As You Earn. Yes, the parent PLUS loan borrower still largely remains out in the cold!

Income-Based Repayment (IBR), a Second-Generation Repayment Plan

Income-Based Repayment reduces your monthly installment to 15 percent of discretionary income. This repayment schedule offers borrowers partial loan forgiveness after twenty-five years (300 qualified payments).[28]

How does Sam's monthly installment calculate under the Income-Based Repayment plan?

Income-Based Repayment (IBR) Plan

Loan Type	Disbursement	% Weight	Installment	Accrued i	Subsidy	Outstanding i	Payoff Bal.
DLUNST	08/15/14	7.42%	$7.12	$8.10		$0.98	$2,116.21
DLSTFD	08/15/14	19.31%	$18.51	$21.07	$2.55	$0.00	$5,500.00
DLUNST	08/18/13	7.63%	$7.31	$6.89		$0.00	$2,171.78
DLSTFD	08/18/13	19.68%	$18.87	$17.79	$0.00	$0.00	$5,605.64
DLUNST	08/20/12	8.56%	$8.21	$13.63		$5.42	$2,449.29
DLSTFD	08/20/12	16.06%	$15.40	$12.79	$0.00	$0.00	$4,572.83
DLUNST	08/15/11	9.04%	$8.67	$14.39		$5.73	$2,586.80
DLSTFD	08/15/11	12.29%	$11.78	$9.78	$0.00	$0.00	$3,498.00
Total		100.00%	$95.86	$104.43	$2.55	$12.13	$28,500.56

(Assumes a 30 day month)

Income-Based Repayment Eligibility Requirements
Both federal direct loans and Federal Family Education Loans (FFEL) are eligible.

You must have a partial financial hardship.[29]

The Math Explained:
Sam's discretionary income is $2,110.33 - $1471.25 = $639.08.
His Income-Based Repayment monthly installment is 15% x $639.08 (.15 x $639.08) = $95.86.

The Key Takeaways:

√ The total monthly installment of $95.86 is allocated in payment to each individual loan in the portfolio by its percentage weight of the total portfolio (i.e., $7.12 = $95.86 x 7.42% where 7.42% = $2,114.25/$28,482.41).

√ The interest subsidy is only available to Income-Based Repayment plan participants during years one through three. The interest subsidy may range from 0 percent to 100 percent depending on the total required monthly installment (i.e., 12.12% = $2.55/$21.07).

√ Your credit score may be negatively impacted because of negative amortization.

Caution

Income-driven Repayment Annual Recertification Requirement
All income-driven repayment plans require that you recertify your income and family size (submit a new application and proof of income) each year prior to the plan anniversary date. Fail to

meet this annual deadline and an interest capitalization penalty will be assessed. The Income-Based Repayment plan has the harshest penalty among all income-driven repayment plans for failing to recertify annually: 100 percent of *outstanding interest will capitalize* (added to your current outstanding balance).[30] Ouch!

Income-Based Repayment Eligible Loans
Direct Stafford Loans:
- Direct Unsubsidized Stafford (DLUNST)
- Direct Subsidized Stafford (DLSTFD)
- Direct PLUS loans for graduates or professionals (DLPLGB)

Direct Consolidation Loans (cannot contain any parent PLUS loans):
- Direct Unsubsidized Consolidation (DLUCNS)
- Direct Subsidized Consolidation (DLSCNS)

FFEL Stafford Loans:
- FFEL Unsubsidized Stafford (UNSTFD)
- FFEL Subsidized Stafford (STFFRD)

FFEL PLUS Loans for graduates or professionals (PLUSGB)
FFEL Consolidation Loans (cannot contain any parent PLUS loans)
- FFEL Unsubsidized Consolidation (UNCNS)
- FFEL Subsidized Consolidation (SUBCNS)[31]

Income-Contingent Repayment (ICR), a First-Generation Repayment Plan

Income-Contingent Repayment reduces your required monthly installment to the lesser of 20 percent of discretionary income or your required payment under a twelve-year fixed repayment schedule, adjusted by an income percentage factor. This repayment schedule offers borrowers partial loan forgiveness after twenty-five years (300 qualified payments). Unlike other income-driven repayment schedules, all borrowers qualify regardless of their level of income (i.e., you do not have to prove a partial financial hardship [PFH]).[32]

What is Sam's monthly installment under the Income-Contingent Plan?

Income Contingent Repayment (ICR) Plan

Loan Type	Disbursement	% Weight	Installment	Accrued i	Subsidy	Outstanding i	Payoff Bal.
DLUNST	08/15/14	7.42%	$16.77	$8.10		$0.00	$2,105.58
DLSTFD	08/15/14	19.31%	$43.62	$21.07	None under ICR	$0.00	$5,477.44
DLUNST	08/18/13	7.63%	$17.23	$6.89		$0.00	$2,161.86
DLSTFD	08/18/13	19.68%	$44.47	$17.79	None under ICR	$0.00	$5,580.04
DLUNST	08/20/12	8.56%	$19.34	$13.63		$0.00	$2,432.74
DLSTFD	08/20/12	16.06%	$36.29	$12.79	None under ICR	$0.00	$4,551.94
DLUNST	08/15/11	9.04%	$20.43	$14.39		$0.00	$2,569.32
DLSTFD	08/15/11	12.29%	$27.76	$9.78	None under ICR	$0.00	$3,482.02
Total		100.00%	$225.90	$104.43	$0.00	$0.00	$28,360.94

(Assumes a 30 day month)

The Math Explained:
The steps to determine Sam's required payment are as follows:

1. Total the outstanding balance of Sam's eligible federal direct loans:

Loan Type	Disbursement	Original Bal.	Current Bal.	i Rate	Outstanding i	Payoff
DLUNST	08/15/2014	$2,000.00	$2,114.25	4.66%	$0.00	$2,114.25
DLSTFD	08/15/2014	$5,500.00	$5,500.00	4.66%	$0.00	$5,500.00
DLUNST	08/18/2013	$2,000.00	$2,172.20	3.86%	$0.00	$2,172.20
DLSTFD	08/18/2013	$5,500.00	$5,606.72	3.86%	$0.00	$5,606.72
DLUNST	08/20/2012	$2,000.00	$2,438.45	6.80%	$0.00	$2,438.45
DLSTFD	08/20/2012	$4,500.00	$4,575.44	3.40%	$0.00	$4,575.44
DLUNST	08/15/2011	$2,000.00	$2,575.35	6.80%	$0.00	$2,575.35
DLSTFD	08/15/2011	$3,500.00	$3,500.00	3.40%	$0.00	$3,500.00
Total		$27,000.00	$28,482.41		$0.00	$28,482.41

Sam's current payoff balance is: $28,482.41.

2. Calculate Sam's total monthly installment assuming a twelve-year fixed repayment schedule using this formula:

INCOME-DRIVEN REPAYMENT—THE RAGE!

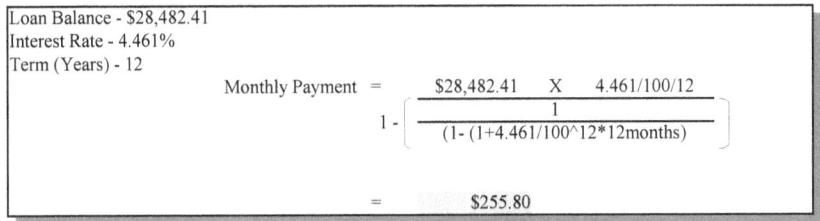

or you may calculate the above in Excel as follows:

	Column A	B
Row 2	Current Balance	$28,482.41
3	Rate	4.461
4	Term (Yrs)	12
5	Payment (Monthly)	=B$2*($B$3/100/12)/(1-(1/(1+$B$3/100/12)^($B$4*12)))

The result is:

Loan Type	Disbursement	Current Bal.	Payoff Bal.	Rate	Term (in Years)	Installment
DLUNST	08/15/14	$2,114.25	$2,114.25	4.66%	12	$19.20
DLSTFD	08/15/14	$5,500.00	$5,500.00	4.66%	12	$49.94
DLUNST	08/18/13	$2,172.20	$2,172.20	3.86%	12	$18.87
DLSTFD	08/18/13	$5,606.72	$5,606.72	3.86%	12	$48.71
DLUNST	08/20/12	$2,438.45	$2,438.45	6.80%	12	$24.82
DLSTFD	08/20/12	$4,575.44	$4,575.44	3.40%	12	$38.74
DLUNST	08/15/11	$2,575.35	$2,575.35	6.80%	12	$26.21
DLSTFD	08/15/11	$3,500.00	$3,500.00	3.40%	12	$29.63
Total		$28,482.41	$28,482.41			**$256.12**

3. Locate the corresponding *income percentage factor* for 2015 that corresponds to Sam's annual gross income level of $25,324 ($2,110.33 x 12 = $25,324) in the table below:

INCOME PERCENTAGE FACTOR for 2015			
Single		Married/Head of Household	
Income	Percentage Factor	Income	Percentage Factor
$11,150	55.00	$11,150	50.52
$15,342	57.79	$17,593	56.68
$19,741	60.57	$20,965	59.56
$24,240	66.23	$27,408	67.79
$28,537	71.89	$33,954	75.22
$33,954	80.33	$42,648	87.61
$42,648	88.77	$53,487	100.00
$53,488	100.00	$64,331	100.00
$64,331	100.00	$80,596	109.40
$77,318	111.80	$107,695	125.00
$99,003	123.50	$145,638	140.60
$140,221	141.20	$203,682	150.00
$160,776	150.00	$332,833	200.00
$286,370	200.00		

Source: Federal Register, vol. 80, no. 57. Wednesday, March 25, 2015, Notices. www.ifap.cd.gov/fregisters/attachments/FR032515.pdf

Unfortunately, there is not an exact match for Sam's income level of $25,324 found in the table, and we cannot easily determine the income percentage factor for 2015. Therefore, we must use a method known as linear interpolation (steps four through nine).

Note: If we were fortunate to find Sam's exact income level of $25,324 listed in the table, we would simply multiply the corresponding income percentage factor associated with Sam's income by the result in step two. Then skip steps four through ten, below, and proceed directly to step eleven. Compare the two results. The lesser of the two figures is Sam's monthly Income-Contingent Repayment installment.

4. Identify the nearest income that is less than $25,324 and the next highest income greater than $25,324. These dollar amounts are $24,240 and $28,537. Calculate their difference: $28,537 - $24,240 = $4,297. This figure is referred to as the *income interval* at $4,297.

5. Locate the percentage factors for these two income levels and subtract their difference (same row, adjacent column, in the income percentage table above): 71.89% - 66.23% = 5.66%. This percentage figure is referred to as the income percentage factor *interval* at 5.66%.

6. Locate the closest income in the table that is less than Sam's actual income and subtract this figure from Sam's income of $25,324: $25,324 - $24,240 = $1,084.

7. Divide the result in step six by the income interval derived in step four: $1,084 ÷ $4,297 = .252.

8. Multiply the result in step seven by the result in step five: .252 x 5.66% = 1.42%.

9. Add the result in step eight to the lower of the two income percentage factors used in step five. The result is Sam's income percentage factor (derived through linear interpolation): 1.42% + 66.23% = 67.65% (*rounded to the nearest hundredth*).

10. Multiply Sam's twelve-year fixed monthly installment calculated in step two by the result in step nine: $256.12 x 67.65% = $173.26.

2015 POVERTY GUIDELINES FOR THE 48 CONTIGUOUS STATES & D.C.			
Family Size	Annual Poverty Guidelines	100% of Annual Poverty Guideline	Monthly
1	$11,770	$11,770	$980.83
2	15,930	15,930	1,327.50
3	20,090	20,090	1,674.17
4	24,250	24,250	2,020.83
5	28,410	28,410	2,367.50
6	32,570	32,570	2,714.17
7	36,730	36,730	3,060.83
8	40,890	40,890	3,407.50
For families/households with more than 8 persons, add $4,160 for each additional person.			

Source: HHS.gov

11. Calculate Sam's discretionary income (discretionary income for the purpose of income contingent repayment is AGI minus the current year HHS poverty guideline figure for family size and State of residence, *unadjusted at 100%*). Multiply the result by 20 percent and divide by twelve (months): $25,324 - $11,770 = $13,544 x .20 = $2,710.80 ÷ 12 = $225.90.

12. The lesser of $173.26 (step ten result) or $225.90 is Sam's monthly Income-Contingent Repayment installment. His monthly Income-Contingent Repayment installment is $173.26. [33]

The Key Takeaways:

√ The total monthly installment of $173.26 is allocated in payment to each individual loan in the portfolio by its percentage weight of the total portfolio (i.e., $16.77 = $225.90 x 7.42% where 7.42% = $2,114.25/$28,482.41).

√ Income-Contingent Repayment participants do not receive a subsidy during years one through three.

√ If your calculated monthly installment is not sufficient to satisfy the interest that accrues, the outstanding interest is capitalized annually. Capitalization of interest cannot exceed more than 10 percent of the original loan balance. Once this maximum is reached, interest will continue to accrue but will no longer be capitalized.

√ Your credit score may be negatively impacted because of negative amortization. Negative amortization results when a monthly installment payment is too small to cover the monthly interest accrual on a loan and your loan balance moves in a negative direction (increases instead of decreases).

Income-Contingent Repayment Eligibility Requirements
Only federal direct loans are eligible.[34]

Income-Contingent Repayment Eligible Loans
Direct Stafford Loans:
- Direct Unsubsidized Stafford (DLUNST)
- Direct Subsidized Stafford (DLSTFD)

Direct PLUS Loans for graduates or professionals (DLPLGB)
Direct Consolidation Loans (must contain direct loans with the student as the borrower *only*):
- Direct Unsubsidized Consolidation (DLUCNS)
- Direct Subsidized Consolidation (DLSCNS)

> Note: Direct Consolidation loans issued, on or after July 1, 2006, to repay direct loan parent PLUS loans *only*, or to repay FFEL parent PLUS loans *only*, or to repay *both* direct loan and FFEL parent PLUS loans together, become eligible.[35]

An Alternative Income Repayment Schedule:

Income-Sensitive Repayment Plan

Only FFEL Program loans are eligible. The plan offers reduced payments limited to the *greater of* 4 percent of gross monthly income[36] (varies depending on the servicer or lender) or thirty-one days of interest accrual. Borrowers may participate for a total of five- to fifteen years depending on the servicer or lender.[37]

Sam is ineligible for Income-Sensitive repayment. His loans are not FFEL Program loans.

Instead let's use as an example a borrower age fifty-nine with a family size of one. We assume a gross monthly income limit of 4 percent:
- Gross monthly income = $1,750.00.
- FFEL loan total outstanding balance = $9,873.41.

- Fixed loan interest rate = 6.8%.
- Current standard ten-year fixed monthly installment = $113.62.

The borrower's Income-Sensitive repayment plan calculation is as follows:

Step 1: Gross monthly income = $1,750.00.

Step 2: Calculate the total monthly interest accrual for all eligible loan(s) = $57.00 ($9,873.41 x .068 = $671.39/365 days = $1.83 per day interest accrual multiplied by 31 maximum days in a month).

Step 3: Calculate 4 percent of gross monthly income = $1,750.00 x .04 = $70.00.

Step 4: The greater of $57.00 (step two result) or $70.00 is the borrower's monthly Income-Sensitive installment. The monthly Income-Sensitive installment is = $70.00.

Note: Some servicers or lenders may apply a debt to income ratio to determine percentage of gross income. Contact your loan servicer for details.

Income-Sensitive Eligibility Requirements
Only Federal Family Education Loans (FFEL) are eligible.[38]

Income-Sensitive Eligible Loans
FFEL Stafford Loans
- FFEL Unsubsidized Stafford (UNSTFD)
- FFEL Subsidized Stafford (STFFRD)

FFEL PLUS Loans for graduates or professionals (PLUSGB)
FFEL Consolidation Loans (may contain FFEL parent PLUS loans)
- FFEL Unsubsidized Consolidation (UNCNS)
- FFEL Subsidized Consolidation (SUBCNS)[39]

Eventually, the Income-Sensitive repayment schedule will be phased-out as outstanding balances on older FFEL Program loans are satisfied.

CHAPTER 4

Teacher Loan Forgiveness

I am a teacher. I was denied my teacher loan forgiveness. I want to know, why!

—Anonymous

Congress enacted the Teacher Loan Forgiveness (TLF) program as an incentive to attract talented and qualified individuals to teach in designated Department of Education, low-income school districts—Title I schools. Qualify and you may be awarded either $5,000 or $17,500 in student loan forgiveness.[40]

Do I qualify?
There are six general eligibility criteria you must satisfy in order to qualify for the TLF program award:

- Work in a Title I designated school district or school during your first year as a teacher.
- Teach full-time.
- Teach at an elementary or secondary school or an educational service agency.

- Teach at least five consecutive and complete academic years.
- Teach in a subject matter that is relevant to your major *or* as a "highly qualified" math, science, or special education educator.
- Carry no outstanding balance on a Direct Loan or FFEL Program loan on October 1, 1998, or on the date that you obtained a Direct Loan or FFEL Program loan after October 1, 1998. The loan (s) must have been disbursed prior to the completion of the fifth academic year at a qualified school.[40]

Is my school a Title I school?
A Title I (reads as *one* as in Roman numeral I) designation is awarded a school or even an entire school district if the school or district's total student enrollment base exceeds 30 percent low-income students. Each year the US Department of Education compiles a directory of Title I designated schools. The title of this annual directory is the *Annual Directory of Designated Low-Income Schools for Teacher Cancellation Benefits*. You may access this directory electronically at *www.tcli.ed.gov*.

The additional funds provided the school district under this classification are in accordance with the Title I of the Elementary and Secondary Education Act of 1965 and any amendments.

Full-Time Status as a Teacher
This standard is established by your respective state government. If your employer's standards for a full-time teacher conflict with that of the federal government's definition of full time for all classifications of employment—currently thirty or more hours per

week—then, generally speaking, your employer's classification will take precedence. If you perform qualified teaching services on a part-time basis and for more than one qualified school or agency and your combined total hours worked for each employer equals or exceeds the required hours necessary to be classified as a full-time teacher, then generally speaking, and for the purpose of the TLF program, you will have satisfied this full-time status requirement.[41]

Elementary or Secondary School or an Educational Service Agency

An elementary school may be a public or a nonprofit private school. A secondary school may be a public or a nonprofit private school. An educational service agency is a regional public multiservice agency (not a private entity) that is authorized by state statute to develop, manage, and provide services or programs to local educational agencies (i.e., public schools).[42]

Five Consecutive and Complete Academic Years

Most state laws consider a complete school year as nine months of instruction. If your school or agency provides year-round instruction, a minimum of nine months service is necessary to be considered a complete academic year. You may combine two consecutive half years and receive credit as one complete year as long as both half years fall within the same twelve-month period. If you were unable to complete an academic year, that year may be counted if:

You completed at least a half year of teaching services *and* your employer granted you credit for a complete academic year on the basis of salary increases, tenure and retirement, *and* the reason that you were unable to complete the entire year of teaching was due to either a pursuit of continued higher education studies on at least a half-time status *and* in a subject area of study considered to enhance your future performance as a teacher, *or* you had a medical condition covered under the Family and Medical Leave Act of 1993 (FMLA).[43]

Note: A half year does not include summer sessions.

What makes a teacher "qualified" or "highly qualified"?
To be considered a qualified teacher at a public elementary or secondary school, a teacher must:

- Hold a full state certification or pass the state's teacher licensing exam.
- Be licensed to teach in the state.
- Meet the state's minimum charter school law if she or he is a public charter schoolteacher.
- Pass competency tests recognized by five or more states, if he or she is a private nonprofit schoolteacher, and achieve a score on each test that equals or exceeds the average passing score for those five states.

Qualified teachers may receive up to $5,000 in loan forgiveness. A *highly qualified* teacher must meet all of the above criteria and be a full-time teacher of mathematics, science, or special education. Highly qualified teachers may receive up to $17,500 of loan forgiveness.

May I be considered both "qualified" and "highly qualified"?
Yes. If you already qualified and have received a service award for $5,000 in teacher loan forgiveness for five consecutive years, you may also reapply for an additional teacher loan forgiveness award of $12,500. You must be accredited as highly qualified *and* you must provide an additional five years of service.[44]

Note: Contact your assigned loan servicer for a copy of the current Teacher Loan Forgiveness Application.

As an elementary, secondary or educational service agency teacher, may I participate in both TLF and Public Service Loan Forgiveness (PSLF)?
Yes, you may. Keep in mind, however, there is no double counting of service years allowed to qualify for TLF and PSLF (chapter 5). TLF is a separate five-year service period, and PSLF is a separate ten-year service period. Thus you must serve as a teacher for a minimum total of fifteen years to qualify for both programs.[45]

As a teacher, may I forgo TLF and choose to participate only in PSLF?
Yes! If you have a large amount of student loan debt outstanding when you enter your teaching career (as defined above), it may not benefit you greatly if your service award under TLF will provide you only $5,000 of forgiveness. In this case, you may elect to forgo the minimal benefits of TLF and immediately participate in PSLF to have 100 percent of your remaining federal direct loan balances forgiven after ten years of qualified payments.

A few examples of how TLF alone, PSLF alone, or TLF and PSLF combined may greatly benefit you:

TLF only

Imagine for a moment an Arizonian who is certified as a special needs teacher at a designated Title I public school. Soon she will begin her second year of full-time teaching. Her student loans, which are outstanding at $28,000 on a $23,000 salary, qualify her for Pay As You Earn at approximately $44 per month. If she teaches only four more years, she may qualify to have up to $17,500 of her remaining loan balance forgiven.

PSLF only

All is well for a twentysomething who is soon to be a full-time elementary teacher in the great state of New Jersey. Her salary of $58,000 is a great starting salary for a first-year teacher with a master's degree. She has $80,500 in outstanding federal-issued direct loans as student loan debt. Being the intelligent, independent woman she is, she opts to participate in PSLF right away. For her, what importance is $5,000 in TLF in five years when she can be awarded 100 percent loan forgiveness in ten years? Her estimated Pay As You Earn payment is only $336.23 per month—an easily affordable payment on her $58,000 annual salary. In ten years, with all things being equal, she may have more than $40,000 forgiven—tax free!

TLF and PSLF combined

Summer is half over for a twenty-seven-year-old, certified elementary teacher at a public Title I school in Pennsylvania. Working part-time over the summer to supplement her six years of teaching has its advantages. It allows her greater independence and the ability to meet her $600 monthly payment on her $55,000 outstanding balance of her federal direct consolidation loan. Skeptical that Teacher Loan Forgiveness and better yet Public Service Loan Forgiveness is "for real," she methodically makes her lofty monthly payments on her student loans on a $45,000 salary (teaching full-time and working part-time over the summer at a golf course). If she applies, she may already qualify for $5,000 of forgiveness under the TLF program. Better yet, she has most likely already earned one year's worth of service and payment credit toward her PSLF program. Even better, her payments will now have been lowered to approximately $200 per month under the Pay As You Earn repayment plan, and she is well on her way to having over 50 percent of her outstanding loan balance entirely forgiven.

CHAPTER 5

Public Service Loan Forgiveness

"Wait ... What? I can have my student loans totally forgiven?"
[Response] "This is right."
"Woo! I am sooo happy right now! I thought I was going to have to be poor, forever!"

—Anonymous

No matter what size your loan balance reads today ...

Current Balance: $37,500.00

or ...

Current Balance: $129,690.00

or even ...

Current Balance: $452,000.00

you may qualify to have your entire remaining loan balance(s) forgiven after only ten years!

Public Service Loan Forgiveness (PSLF)

What is Public Service Loan Forgiveness (PSLF)?

The Public Service Loan Forgiveness (PSLF) program targets *only* full-time, government employees and nonprofit employees (full-time Peace Corps or AmeriCorps participants also qualify). The program's sole intent is to encourage (expand) future generations of college graduates to pursue fields of study or career paths in government or nonprofit organizations. After only ten years of qualified public service, this program offers total student loan forgiveness on any balance that remains on your federal student loan account.[46] Parent holders of parent PLUS loan(s) may also qualify for forgiveness if the parent, who is considered the borrower in this instance, works full-time in public service. (see chapter 7).

Public Service Loan Forgiveness (PSLF) was enacted by Congress and signed by President Obama's part of the College Cost Reduction Act of 2007, a subcomponent piece of legislation nestled within the Affordable Care Act (i.e., Obamacare).[47] Any future legislative changes to this act will, of course, face strong political headwinds. Any alterations to *the promise* of total loan forgiveness through participation in this program will require congressional passage and a presidential signature.

Note: President Obama's 2015 Budget Proposal (published March 10, 2014) contained a request to cap the total amount of public service loan forgiveness at $57,500 for public-sector employees.⁴⁸ Congress never passed this budget.

Do I qualify?

There is a six-point eligibility test that you must meet to qualify, participate in, and be awarded *total* loan forgiveness under PSLF. The six eligibility hurdles are:

- Qualified employment
- Approved Employee Certification Form
- Eligible loan (s)
- Eligible repayment plan
- Ten years of qualified, separate monthly payments (120) after October 2007.
- Final Forgiveness Application (The earliest that final forgiveness may occur is October 2017. Therefore, the Department of Education has not yet made this application available for public dissemination.⁴⁹)

Employment/Employer:
You must be considered a *full-time* employee according to your employer or work greater than thirty hours per week according to the government definition of full time. You also must work in *either* a government (federal, state, local, or municipality) or a nonprofit entity that is designated as a tax-exempt organization by the Internal Revenue Service under Section 501(c)(3) of the Internal Revenue Code (IRC) or a private nonprofit entity that is not a tax-exempt organization under Section 501(c)(3) of the IRC but provides special public services.[50]

To determine if your current organization is a nonprofit 501(c)(3), simply access http://www.irs.gov/app/pub-78 *or* http://www.irs.gov/uac/501-tax-stats-exemp-organizations-business-master-file-extract-(EO-BMF). You may conduct your search at either of these websites by employer name or employer identification number (EIN). You may also contact the current loan servicer, contracted by the Department of Education, to administer *all* PSLF participant accounts.

Full-time employment requirements:
Your qualified employer must consider you a full-time employee. *And* you must meet the government test for full-time employment of a minimum thirty hours per week, or at least an annualized average of thirty hours per week if under a contractual work agreement. Or if you are a part-time employee but work for multiple qualified employers *simultaneously* and on a part-time basis, you may qualify if, your *combined hours* for *all* qualified employers totals thirty hours or more.[51]

Note: The PSLF program was enacted by a Democratic-led majority in both the Senate and the House of Representatives. It is not surprising then that this liberal-based majority saw fit to disqualify from PSLF participation any and all employment that constitutes religious instruction or proselytizing. Let's consider a few examples based *solely* on employment criteria:

Qualifies:
- Full-time police officer for a local city.
- Staff surgeon for a nonprofit Catholic hospital (although the hospital has a religious affiliation, the surgeon's responsibilities do not).
- Part-time firefighter for the city who also works simultaneously as a part-time EMT for a local county hospital. This worker may qualify but only if the cumulative hours worked on both jobs exceed an annualized average that is equal to or greater than thirty hours per week.

Does not qualify:
- Minister employed by a Presbyterian church. Why not? The minister is actively engaged in religious instructional activities.
- Full-time consultant at a for-profit government contractor who provides consulting services to governmental agencies. Why not? The consultant's employer is a for-profit company.
- Substitute public schoolteacher, not under a contract, who only works nine months of a full calendar year. Why not? As a substitute teacher, the annualized average hours worked will fall short of the thirty-hour-per-week average when calculated over a twelve-month period.

- Public schoolteacher with twenty years of service who plans to retire in 2017. Why not? Although the teacher qualifies to participate in PSLF, this teacher will only tally nine years toward a qualified service period until retirement in 2017. Since the PSLF program only counts service years and payments from 2008 and beyond, this person will fall short of the ten-year service period and qualified payment requirement under PSLF.

Employment Certification Form (ECF)

You must have an authorized official at your place of employment certify that you meet the eligibility requirements for the Public Service Loan Forgiveness (PSLF) program. This requires your authorized official to complete, sign, and then submit, on your behalf, an Employment Certification Form (ECF). Once the PSLF-assigned loan servicer (appointed by the Department of Education under a renewable contract agreement to administer PSLF on behalf of qualified borrower participants), receives the completed ECF, it will review the application for completeness, eligibility, and approval. Once approval is granted, your ECF will remain on file.[52]

An important item to consider about the ECF:
Although you are not required to submit an ECF form until you submit your final application for forgiveness, it would serve you well to submit a form each year to properly document your work history. This is especially important if you have multiple employers throughout your ten-year work history. The burden of proof always rests on the borrower's shoulders in these instances.

The PSLF Employment Certification Form (ECF) is available at: https://studentaid.ed.gov/sa/repay-loans/forgiveness-cancellation/public-service

Since no one will actually qualify for loan forgiveness under the PSLF program until after October 1, 2017, the PSLF final forgiveness application remains uncirculated.

Eligible Loan Types
Only federal direct loans issued under the William D. Ford Federal Loan Program are deemed eligible.[53]

You may still be eligible if you were issued a Federal Family Education Loan (FFEL) or loans made under other federal student loan programs that were consolidated or can be consolidated into a new Direct Consolidation Loan. Then only the payments made on this *new* consolidated loan will qualify for PSLF.[54] I recommend that you contact the Department of Education-assigned PSLF loan servicer to better address your individual options for this important eligibility maneuver.

You may also access *www.nslds.ed.gov* to identify your loan by its type: either a Federal Direct Loan Program (FDLP) loan or a Federal Family Education Loan (FFEL) Program loan.

Repayment Schedules
Eligible Repayment Schedules:
- Standard ten-year fixed payment
- *Most* income-driven repayment schedules: Pay As You Earn (PAYE), Revised Pay As You Earn (REPAYE), Income-Based Repayment (IBR), and Income-Contingent Repayment (ICR)

Ineligible Repayment Schedules:

- The ten-year graduated and all extended-term schedules (i.e., the twelve-year, fifteen-year, twenty-year, twenty-five year, and thirty-year repayment schedules)[55]

It doesn't take a math genius to figure out that, if you elect to participate in the standard ten-year repayment schedule to satisfy your 120 qualified, on-time payments, you will have most likely satisfied your loan balance yourself. There will be no balance left to be forgiven! Although this may be true, consider this hypothetical example:

For two years a full-time nurse at a public, nonprofit hospital has been making student loan payments on her direct loans under the standard ten-year repayment plan schedule. If, just as of today, she were to learn of her PSLF eligibility, potentially *all* of her previous payments would still count towards the 120 qualified payments. However, she may want to consider a switch to an income-driven repayment plan to effectively reduce any future out-of-pocket expense and to maximize any PSLF service forgiveness award over the time that remains.

One hundred twenty qualified, monthly payments (ten years)
There are five primary factors that determine whether or not a payment under the PSLF program is considered a qualified payment or not.

1. Only payments made to a qualified repayment plan after October 1, 2007, qualify.
2. A payment must post (be credited) to your student loan account no earlier than five calendar days *prior to* or

fifteen calendar days *after* your due date to count as a qualified payment.
3. All payments must be separate payments (i.e., if your installment payment is $100 per month, but you decide to pay $400, you will only receive credit for one month).
4. Likewise, for a payment to count as qualified, it must fully satisfy the monthly installment amount or a number of separate partial payments in the month combined together must satisfy the monthly installment amount.
5. Payments *do not* have to be consecutive to receive credit.

Perhaps the biggest misnomer of all: What happens if I miss a payment? Do I reset to year zero? No! You simply pick up where you last left off. This applies to both payments and also employment service periods.

Elective payments made during periods of deferment or forbearance are not considered scheduled payments, and therefore, they do not count as qualified payments toward PSLF.[56]

Final Application for Forgiveness

The first date that someone can actually apply for loan forgiveness under the PSLF program will not occur until October 1, 2017. The final application for PSLF is a document that is only referenced by the Department of Education at the time of this writing. This document remains uncirculated for public use. It also must be noted that you have to be working full-time for a nonprofit or government entity at the time you submit this final forgiveness application *and* at the time you are awarded total forgiveness. Of course, some people may choose to delay submission of their

ECF until this final stage (the end of ten service years). Prudent participants would elect to submit their ECF each and every year so their service qualification is properly documented each and every year. This proves especially important if you have worked for multiple employers over the ten-year time period. Lastly, no accommodation for partial forgiveness is granted under PSLF. It is either 100 percent qualification or nothing!

A Positive Example of the Benefits of PSLF Participation

A hypothetical social worker in Alabama loves working with children with disabilities at a nonprofit. Her modest income of $24,000 per year as a single professional doesn't leave her much room to support her near $54,000 in student loans. She qualifies for a $0.00 monthly payment on a Pay As You Earn repayment plan. Better yet, her $0.00 monthly payment will count towards her 120 qualified payment requirement under PSLF.

Additional Positive Examples of PSLF Participation

Pursuing higher education is the choice for this hypothetical married couple, who both have PhDs. Even though they are secure with government research positions, the husband decides its time to pursue yet another PhD. Never mind the $800,000-plus combined student loan debt they both carry; one is not complete with only one PhD. With only a joint gross annual income of $78,000, they will struggle to support the $471 per month combined payment on their Income-Based Repayment plans. This qualified payment is barely enough to cover two months of annual interest accrual on their combined outstanding loan balances. How will they ever repay these debts? No worries, PSLF will forgive this intelligent couple their debts in just 120 qualified payments.

Imagine a physician with a nonworking spouse and four young children, who decides that a new dream home to fulfill his wife's wishes is most important. As an employee of a nonprofit hospital, with an annualized salary of $180,000, the physician is eligible to participate in PSLF. An Income-Based Repayment plan offers this physician a lower alternative repayment commitment on a $320,000 federal student loan balance with shaved payments at only $230 per month. Forgiveness will occur on any balance that remains in ten short years.

A Not-So-Positive Example: the Tax Penalty of Marriage and Filing Jointly with PSLF Participation

Recall our hypothetical social worker and fast-forward to a year later. Her annual renewal notice has just arrived in the mail. Her new monthly payment has jumped to $540 per month from $0.00. Why? Well, she got married. Not only did she get married, but she also filed taxes as married filing jointly for the latest tax season. That's unfortunate for her. Now her monthly payments must be based on her new *combined gross income* (AGI) figure. She has just experienced the marriage penalty with PSLF.

Her options: Make an attempt to satisfy this higher required payment and remain a qualified PSLF participant over the next twelve months; take a year off from PSLF participation with plans to reenter the program after changing her tax status to married filing separately, which currently allows a lower payment based solely on her income while in a larger family size of two; or simply exit PSLF participation altogether with no future plans to reenter.

CHAPTER 6

Deferment and Forbearance—A Borrower's Privilege?

"I'd like to defer my loans … please."
[Response] "Do you wish to apply for a deferment or request a forbearance?"
"I don't know. What's the difference? I just want to postpone my payments for a while, please."

—Anonymous

Yes! The federal government (as lender of the taxpayer's money) allows you to postpone your payments for temporary periods of time on your student loans. This is your borrower privilege—a major advantage of having borrowed student funds from the federal government. How many other creditors (lenders) can you think of that will allow you to temporarily postpone the payments on your debt until you find it more financially convenient to pay on it? Not many. Perhaps none!

A borrower once remarked, "It must be nice to have a job where you can tell people it is okay if you can't meet your loan commitment for the next three months."

Why does the federal government grant this nicety? It's a moneymaker for the federal government (taxpayer). A nicety for you, the borrower, but also a moneymaker for the government. This short-term privilege does not come without some level of long-run consequence however.

Deferment and Forbearance

There are two traditional types of postponement of payment options for federal student loan borrowers. They are deferment and forbearance. While both offer you a way to postpone your payments for a set period of time, they do differ greatly in their qualification requirements. Most importantly, they differ in how your interest accrual is treated. If you seek to postpone your payments due to undue hardship, your decision hierarchy should *always* be deferment first, forbearance second!

Postponement Hierarchy

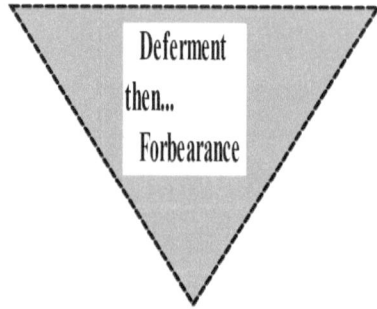

Here Is Why

If you elect to postpone your payments through deferment, the government (taxpayer) subsidizes (*pays*) the accrued interest on subsidized loans, but it will not subsidize the accrued interest on *any* unsubsidized loans, including PLUS loans (i.e., parent, graduate, or professional loans).[57] This is why deferment has more stringent qualification requirements. The subsidy that you will receive is subsidized, ultimately, by someone else's taxpayer dollars, and therefore, you *must* provide documented proof of this temporary financial hardship.

Postponement of payments through forbearance, on the other hand, *will not* qualify for an interest subsidy on any loan types, subsidized or unsubsidized. You may or you may not have to provide proof of your temporary financial hardship to qualify. It simply depends on the type of forbearance you request.

The Five Major Types of Deferment
1. In-school
2. Post-enrollment period (grace)
3. Unemployment
4. Economic hardship
5. Military (active)

In-School Deferment
Maximum time limit: none![58]
Theoretically, you may attend school at least half-time forever! To qualify for in-school deferment, you must be *both* enrolled *and* actively attending at least half-time or greater. "At least half-time" enrollment status typically requires six credit hours in an undergraduate-level program or eight credit hours in a graduate-level program. The school determines your eligibility status as less than half time, half time, three-quarters time, or full time.[59]

Example:

You enroll in July to attend classes during the fall semester with a semester start date of August 25. Even if you have scheduled the classes you plan to take that begin on August 25, you will not qualify for in-school deferment status until August 25. This is the date that you meet both the enrollment and actively attending requirements and not before.

Who reports your in-school status?

Your school's student financial aid department reports your current status. It utilizes one or both competing national databases: National Student Loan Data Systems (NSLDS) at *www.nslds.ed.gov* or National Student Clearinghouse (NSC) at *www.studentclearinghouse.gov*. In turn, your assigned loan servicer will download this electronically submitted data and apply the in-school status to your loan(s).

Note: If you have an income-driven repayment (IDR) plan (i.e., Pay As You Earn or Income-Based Repayment) and your in-school deferment eligibility period overlaps with the initial subsidy period (years one through three) of your income-driven repayment plan, your period of in-school deferment subtracts from this initial three-year subsidy period.[60]

Unemployment Deferment

Maximum time limit: three years (consecutive periods are allowed).[61]

Income limit: none [62] (i.e., you may be working less than thirty hours but earning $100 per hour and you still will qualify).

This type of deferment applies even if you are working less than thirty hours per week but are actively seeking full-time employment and registered with an employment agency.

Note: If you have an income-driven repayment (IDR) plan (i.e., Pay As You Earn, Revised Pay As You Earn, or Income-Based Repayment plans only) and your qualifying period of unemployment deferment overlaps with the initial subsidy period (years one through three) of your IDR plan, any period of unemployment deferment subsidy *subtracts from* this initial IDR three year subsidy period

Let's consider this simplified version of Sam's portfolio below:

Loan Type	Disbursement	Original Bal.	Current Bal.	*i* Rate	Outstanding *i*	Payoff
DLUNST	08/15/2014	$2,000.00	$2,114.25	4.66%	$0.00	$2,114.25
DLSTFD	08/15/2014	$5,500.00	$5,500.00	4.66%	$0.00	$5,500.00
DLUNST	08/18/2013	$2,000.00	$2,172.20	3.86%	$0.00	$2,172.20
DLSTFD	08/18/2013	$5,500.00	$5,606.72	3.86%	$0.00	$5,606.72
DLUNST	08/20/2012	$2,000.00	$2,438.45	6.80%	$0.00	$2,438.45
DLSTFD	08/20/2012	$4,500.00	$4,575.44	3.40%	$0.00	$4,575.44
DLUNST	08/15/2011	$2,000.00	$2,575.35	6.80%	$0.00	$2,575.35
DLSTFD	08/15/2011	$3,500.00	$3,500.00	3.40%	$0.00	$3,500.00
Total		$27,000.00	$28,482.41		$0.00	$28,482.41

If Sam elected either Pay As You Earn or Income-Based Repayment as his underlying repayment schedule and qualified for a deferment in his first month of repayment, how would this impact Sam's subsidy period during years one through three?

Pay As You Earn (PAYE): (see chapter 3)

Unemployment Deferment and Pay–As–You–Earn (PAYE) Repayment

Loan Type	Installment	Accrued *i*	Subsidy	Outstanding *i*	Payoff Bal.
DLUNST	$0.00	$8.10		$8.10	$2,122.35
DLSTFD	$0.00	$21.07	100% subsidy of $21.07	$0.00	$5,500.00
DLUNST	$0.00	$6.89		$6.89	$2,179.09
DLSTFD	$0.00	$17.79	100% subsidy of $17.79	$0.00	$5,606.72
DLUNST	$0.00	$13.63		$13.63	$2,452.08
DLSTFD	$0.00	$12.79	100% subsidy of $12.79	$0.00	$4,575.44
DLUNST	$0.00	$14.39		$14.39	$2,589.74
DLSTFD	$0.00	$9.78	100% subsidy of $9.78	$0.00	$3,500.00
Total	**$0.00**	**$104.43**	**Total Subsidy is $61.43**	**$43.01**	**$28,525.42**

(Assumes a 30 day month)

Income-Based Repayment (IBR): (see chapter 3)

Unemployment Deferment and Income-Based Repayment (IBR)

Loan Type	Installment	Accrued *i*	Subsidy	Outstanding *i*	Payoff Bal.
DLUNST	$0.00	$8.10		$8.10	$2,122.35
DLSTFD	$0.00	$21.07	100% subsidy of $21.07	$0.00	$5,500.00
DLUNST	$0.00	$6.89		$6.89	$2,179.09
DLSTFD	$0.00	$17.79	100% subsidy of $17.79	$0.00	$5,606.72
DLUNST	$0.00	$13.63		$13.63	$2,452.08
DLSTFD	$0.00	$12.79	100% subsidy of $12.79	$0.00	$4,575.44
DLUNST	$0.00	$14.39		$14.39	$2,589.74
DLSTFD	$0.00	$9.78	100% subsidy of $9.78	$0.00	$3,500.00
Total	**$0.00**	**$104.43**	**Total Subsidy is $61.43**	**$43.01**	**$28,525.42**

(Assumes a 30 day month)

Sam will receive a 100 percent interest subsidy on only his subsidized loans during any qualified period of unemployment deferment and as a participant of either Pay As You Earn (including Revised Pay As You Earn) or Income-Based Repayment during years one through three, or during any qualified period beyond years one through three as illustrated above. Sam will also receive a 100 percent interest subsidy on his subsidized loans if Sam were to participate in *any* traditional repayment schedules (i.e. standard ten-year fixed, ten-year graduated, etc.) as illustrated below:

DEFERMENT AND FORBEARANCE—A BORROWER'S PRIVILEGE?

Unemployment Deferment and Standard Ten-Year Fixed Repayment

Loan Type	Installment	Accrued *i*	Subsidy	Outstanding *i*	Payoff Bal.
DLUNST	$0.00	$8.10		$8.10	$2,122.35
DLSTFD	$0.00	$21.07	100% subsidy of $21.07	$0.00	$5,500.00
DLUNST	$0.00	$6.89		$6.89	$2,179.09
DLSTFD	$0.00	$17.79	100% subsidy of $17.79	$0.00	$5,606.72
DLUNST	$0.00	$13.63		$13.63	$2,452.08
DLSTFD	$0.00	$12.79	100% subsidy of $12.79	$0.00	$4,575.44
DLUNST	$0.00	$14.39		$14.39	$2,589.74
DLSTFD	$0.00	$9.78	100% subsidy of $9.78	$0.00	$3,500.00
Totals	$0.00	$104.43	Total Subsidy is $61.43	$43.01	$28,525.42

(Assumes a 30 day month)

As one can quickly see, regardless of Sam's repayment selection choice, his subsidized loans will be treated equally with a 100 percent subsidy.

Economic Hardship Deferment (includes Peace Corps)

Maximum time limit: three years (consecutive periods are allowed).[63] Income limit: A borrower's earnings cannot exceed 150 percent of the annual poverty guidelines as released by the US Department of Health and Human Services (HHS) in the current year (see chapter 3).

If you receive federal or state public assistance or general state assistance you may qualify for economic hardship deferment. Here are some of the current qualifying examples:

- Supplemental Social Security Insurance (SSI)
- Supplemental Security Disability Insurance (SSD)
- Federal Supplemental Nutritional Assistance Program (SNAP)
- Food Stamps Supplemental Nutrition Assistance Program—Women, Infants, and Children (WIC)
- Federal School Lunch Program
- Medicaid

- Temporary Assistance for Needy Families (TANF)
- State Medical Assistance (CHIP)
- State General Public Assistance
- Section 8 Housing Voucher
- Service as a Peace Corp volunteer [64]

For a more complete and current list, contact your assigned loan servicer.

Note: If you have an income-driven repayment (IDR) plan (i.e., Pay As You Earn, Revised Pay As You Earn, or Income-Based Repayment only) and your economic hardship deferment eligibility period overlaps with the initial subsidy period (years one through three) under your IDR plan, then your period of economic hardship deferment subsidy *extends (adds to)* this initial three-year subsidy period. Economic hardship deferment is also the only deferment type that offers borrower credit as a qualified payment during the coverage period.

Let's consider this simplified version of Sam's portfolio below:

Loan Type	Disbursement	Original Bal.	Current Bal.	*i* Rate	Outstanding *i*	Payoff
DLUNST	08/15/2014	$2,000.00	$2,114.25	4.66%	$0.00	$2,114.25
DLSTFD	08/15/2014	$5,500.00	$5,500.00	4.66%	$0.00	$5,500.00
DLUNST	08/18/2013	$2,000.00	$2,172.20	3.86%	$0.00	$2,172.20
DLSTFD	08/18/2013	$5,500.00	$5,606.72	3.86%	$0.00	$5,606.72
DLUNST	08/20/2012	$2,000.00	$2,438.45	6.80%	$0.00	$2,438.45
DLSTFD	08/20/2012	$4,500.00	$4,575.44	3.40%	$0.00	$4,575.44
DLUNST	08/15/2011	$2,000.00	$2,575.35	6.80%	$0.00	$2,575.35
DLSTFD	08/15/2011	$3,500.00	$3,500.00	3.40%	$0.00	$3,500.00
Total		$27,000.00	$28,482.41		$0.00	$28,482.41

If Sam elected either Pay As You Earn, or Income-Based Repayment as his underlying repayment schedule and qualified for a deferment in his first month of repayment, how would this impact Sam's subsidy period during year's one through three?

Pay As You Earn (PAYE):

Economic Hardship Deferment and Pay-As-You-Earn (PAYE) Repayment

Loan Type	Installment	Accrued i	Subsidy	Outstanding i	Payoff Bal.
DLUNST	$0.00	$8.10		$8.10	$2,122.35
DLSTFD	$0.00	$21.07	100% subsidy of $21.07	$0.00	$5,500.00
DLUNST	$0.00	$6.89		$6.89	$2,179.09
DLSTFD	$0.00	$17.79	100% subsidy of $17.79	$0.00	$5,606.72
DLUNST	$0.00	$13.63		$13.63	$2,452.08
DLSTFD	$0.00	$12.79	100% subsidy of $12.79	$0.00	$4,575.44
DLUNST	$0.00	$14.39		$14.39	$2,589.74
DLSTFD	$0.00	$9.78	100% subsidy of $9.78	$0.00	$3,500.00
Total	**$0.00**	104.43	Total Subsidy is $61.43	**$43.01**	**$28,525.42**

(Assumes a 30 day month)

Income-Based Repayment (IBR):

Economic Hardship Deferment and Income-Based Repayment (IBR)

Loan Type	Installment	Accrued i	Subsidy	Outstanding i	Payoff Bal.
DLUNST	$0.00	$8.10		$8.10	$2,122.35
DLSTFD	$0.00	$21.07	100% subsidy of $21.07	$0.00	$5,500.00
DLUNST	$0.00	$6.89		$6.89	$2,179.09
DLSTFD	$0.00	$17.79	100% subsidy of $17.79	$0.00	$5,606.72
DLUNST	$0.00	$13.63		$13.63	$2,452.08
DLSTFD	$0.00	$12.79	100% subsidy of $12.79	$0.00	$4,575.44
DLUNST	$0.00	$14.39		$14.39	$2,589.74
DLSTFD	$0.00	$9.78	100% subsidy of $9.78	$0.00	$3,500.00
Total	**$0.00**	$104.43	Total Subsidy is $61.43	**$43.01**	**$28,525.42**

(Assumes a 30 day month)

Sam will receive a 100 percent interest subsidy on his subsidized loans under Pay As You Earn, Revised Pay As You Earn and Income-Based Repayment, as illustrated above. If Sam had elected to remain in a standard ten-year fixed repayment schedule at repayment outset, he would still receive his 100 percent interest subsidy on the subsidized loans in his portfolio as illustrated below:

Economic Hardship Deferment and Standard Ten-Year Fixed Repayment

Loan Type	Installment	Accrued *i*	Subsidy	Outstanding *i*	Payoff Bal.
DLUNST	$0.00	$8.10		$8.10	$2,122.35
DLSTFD	$0.00	$21.07	100% subsidy of $21.07	$0.00	$5,500.00
DLUNST	$0.00	$6.89		$6.89	$2,179.09
DLSTFD	$0.00	$17.79	100% subsidy of $17.79	$0.00	$5,606.72
DLUNST	$0.00	$13.63		$13.63	$2,452.08
DLSTFD	$0.00	$12.79	100% subsidy of $12.79	$0.00	$4,575.44
DLUNST	$0.00	$14.39		$14.39	$2,589.74
DLSTFD	$0.00	$9.78	100% subsidy of $9.78	$0.00	$3,500.00
Totals	$0.00	$104.43	Total Subsidy is $61.43	$43.01	$28,525.42

(Assumes a 30 day month)

As one can quickly see, regardless of Sam's repayment selection choice, his subsidized loans will be treated equally with a 100 percent subsidy.

Military Duty Deferment

Maximum time limit: none.[65]

Only active military status qualifies. The military duty must be a result of an act of war and carry a named military operation (i.e., Operation Desert Storm), or the result of a national emergency.

Eligible Federal Loans

Federal Direct Loan Program (FDLP) loans—issued from 2002 and beyond:
- Direct Loan Subsidized Stafford (DLSTFD)
- Direct Loan Unsubsidized Stafford (DLUNST)
- Direct PLUS loan issued to a graduate student or professional (DLPLGB)
- Direct PLUS loan issued to a parent for the benefit of a dependent student (DLPLUS)
- Direct Subsidized Consolidation (DLSCNS)
- Direct Unsubsidized Consolidation (DLUNCS)

Federal Family Education Loan (FFEL)—These loans may have been issued prior to 2008:
- FFEL Subsidized Stafford (STFD)
- FFEL Unsubsidized Stafford (UNSTFD)
- FFEL Graduate Plus (PLUSGB)
- FFEL Parent PLUS (PLUS)
- FFEL Subsidized Consolidation (SUBCNS)
- FFEL Unsubsidized Consolidation (UNCNS)[66]

Forbearance

The federal government *does not* pay the interest accrued during any qualified periods of forbearance. This is true even for subsidized loans.

The Two Major Types of Forbearances
Mandatory
Maximum time limit: unlimited.
Discretionary
Maximum time limit: limited.[67]

The Three *Major* Types of *Mandatory* Forbearances
Medical or dental
Department of Defense
National Guard

The Three *Minor* Types of *Mandatory* Forbearances
Teacher Loan Forgiveness
AmeriCorps (national community service)
Disaster

The Two Types of *Discretionary* Forbearances
General Forbearance
Student Loan Debt Burden Forbearance

General Forbearance:
Maximum time limit: three years (consecutive periods are allowed). Income limit: none.[68]

Note: If you have an income-driven repayment (IDR) plan (i.e., Pay As You Earn, Revised Pay As You Earn, or Income-Based Repayment plans only) and your forbearance period overlaps any initial subsidy period (years one through three) of your income-driven repayment plan, you *forfeit* the subsidy during this period of overlap.

Pay As You Earn (PAYE): (see chapter 3)

Forbearances and Pay–As–You Earn (PAYE) Repayment					
Loan Type	Installment	Accrued i	Subsidy	Outstanding i	Payoff Bal.
DLUNST	$0.00	$8.10		$8.10	$2,122.35
DLSTFD	$0.00	$21.07	Forfeits $8.73 subsidy	$21.07	$5,521.07
DLUNST	$0.00	$6.89		$6.89	$2,179.09
DLSTFD	$0.00	$17.79	Forfeits $5.21 subsidy	$17.79	$5,624.51
DLUNST	$0.00	$13.63		$13.63	$2,452.08
DLSTFD	$0.00	$12.79	Forfeits $2.52 subsidy	$12.79	$4,588.23
DLUNST	$0.00	$14.39		$14.39	$2,589.74
DLSTFD	$0.00	$9.78	Forfeits $1.93 subsidy	$9.78	$3,509.78
Total	$0.00	$104.43	Total Lost subsidy - $18.38	$104.43	$28,586.84
(Assumes a 30 day month)					

Income-Based Repayment (IBR): (see chapter 3)

Forbearances and Income-Based Repayment (IBR)

Loan Type	Installment	Accrued i	Subsidy	Outstanding i	Payoff Bal.
DLUNST	$0.00	$8.10		$8.10	$2,122.35
DLSTFD	$0.00	$21.07	Forfeits $2.55 subsidy	$21.07	$5,521.07
DLUNST	$0.00	$6.89		$6.89	$2,179.09
DLSTFD	$0.00	$17.79	$0.00	$17.79	$5,624.51
DLUNST	$0.00	$13.63		$13.63	$2,452.08
DLSTFD	$0.00	$12.79	$0.00	$12.79	$4,588.23
DLUNST	$0.00	$14.39		$14.39	$2,589.74
DLSTFD	$0.00	$9.78	$0.00	$9.78	$3,509.78
Total	**$0.00**	**$104.43**	Total Lost subsidy - $2.55	$104.43	$28,586.84

(Assumes a 30 day month)

If Sam requests a forbearance of his loan payments while participating in a standard ten-year fixed repayment schedule, Sam will not receive an interest subsidy on any of the loans in his portfolio as illustrated below:

Forbearances and Standard 10-Year Fixed Repayment

Loan Type	Installment	Accrued i	Subsidy	Outstanding i	Payoff Bal.
DLUNST	$0.00	$8.10		$8.10	$2,122.35
DLSTFD	$0.00	$21.07	None	$21.07	$5,521.07
DLUNST	$0.00	$6.89		$6.89	$2,179.09
DLSTFD	$0.00	$17.79	None	$17.79	$5,624.51
DLUNST	$0.00	$13.63		$13.63	$2,452.08
DLSTFD	$0.00	$12.79	None	$12.79	$4,588.23
DLUNST	$0.00	$14.39		$14.39	$2,589.74
DLSTFD	$0.00	$9.78	None	$9.78	$3,509.78
Total	**$0.00**	**$104.43**	Total Subsidy is $0.00	$104.43	$28,586.84

(Assumes a 30 day month)

Note: If you have exhausted your three-year period of general (temporary hardship) forbearance time and have yet to consolidate your existing loans, consolidation may benefit you. Consolidation will pay off your existing loans and create a new loan. This new loan will refresh your three years of general forbearance eligibility once again.

Student Loan Debt Burden Forbearance
Maximum time limit: three years (consecutive periods are allowed). Income limit: Yes.

The borrower's total monthly payment on all eligible outstanding federal loans must be greater than 20 percent of the borrower's gross monthly income.[69]

Eligible Loans
Federal Direct Loan Program (FDLP) loans—issued from 2002 and beyond:
- Direct Loan Subsidized Stafford (DLSTFD)
- Direct Loan Unsubsidized Stafford (DLUNST)
- Direct PLUS loan issued to a graduate student or professional (DLPLGB)
- Direct PLUS loan issued to a parent for the benefit of a dependent student (DLPLUS)
- Direct Subsidized Consolidation (DLSCNS)
- Direct Unsubsidized Consolidation (DLUNCS)

Federal Family Education Loan (FFEL)—These loans may have been issued you prior to 2008:
- FFEL Subsidized Stafford (STFD)
- FFEL Unsubsidized Stafford (UNSTFD)
- FFEL Graduate Plus (PLUSGB)
- FFEL Parent PLUS (PLUS)
- FFEL Subsidized Consolidation (SUBCNS)
- FFEL Unsubsidized Consolidation (UNCNS)[70]

Capitalization of Interest
If you elect to not satisfy any accrued interest that accumulated during your elected period of deferment or forbearance, the

unpaid interest that had accrued during this period will capitalize (exceptions exist for certain types of income-driven repayment plans). Capitalize means the interest is added to your current principal balance. This capitalized interest event will cause two things to happen to your loan. First, the daily interest accrual on your loan will *increase.* Second, and more importantly, your monthly installment may also *increase* in order to satisfy this extra interest accrual amount. Under traditional repayment schedules (e.g. Standard 10-year fixed, 10-year graduated and the extended term repayment schedules) this payment increase will automatically appear on subsequent installment bills. Under income-driven repayment, however, this additional daily interest accrual may go largely unnoticed. Why? You may ask? Capitalization of interest will not immediately increase your monthly installment since there has been no change to the three variables that determine your required payment—your income, family size or tax status. What is most likely to occur, however, is greater negative amortization on your total loan balance.

CHAPTER 7

Parent PLUS Loans—"Thank You, Mom and Dad!"

"How can I lower my interest rate on my loans?"
[Response] "You can't."
"Then put me in default right now. I am never going to pay back these loans. There is no sense in waiting. Just put me in default. Right now!"
—Anonymous Parent Borrower

Fifty thousand dollars! This is the average amount that a parent must borrow through the federal government's direct loan program (FDLP) to fund one child's four-year college education, according to 2014 federal student loan data. This $50,000 parent loan figure is roughly two times the average loan balance the student must borrow at $26,000.

Who is the borrower?

As a dad or a mom, you are the borrower. Yes, this Federal Direct PLUS loan is in your name –as a parent – and not in the name of the dependent student. The purpose of this type of loan is to cover the funding gap that still exists after the dependent student has maximized his or her own annual federal loan lending cap. This parent loan will remain in your respective name until it is paid in full or forgiven, or as a result of your own death. Under the FDLP, it is not transferable ever!

Why is such a high rate of interest charged for parent loans?

There is little to no explanation. It appears that Congress has reasoned that someone has to carry the bulk of the funding burden, so why not you, the parent? Simply read the excerpt below and notice the arbitrary language written in the Bipartisan Student Loan Certainty Act of 2013 that grants Congress the ability to set the rates on all newly issued federal direct loans after 2013:

> Federal Parent PLUS loans—the applicable rate of interest shall be equal to the *lesser of* (i) a rate equal to the high yield of the 10-year Treasury note auctioned at the final auction held prior to such June 1 *plus 4.6%;* or (ii) 10.5%.

Now compare this to the add-on rate charged all other student borrowers—undergraduates and graduate students—as depicted below:

Loan Type	Loan Code	High Yield Rate	(+)	Add-On Rate	=	Final Rate
DL Subsized Stafford	DLSTFD	2.237%	(+)	2.05%	=	4.29%
DL Subsized Stafford	DLUNST	2.237%	(+)	2.05%	=	4.29%
DL Graduate	DLPLGB	2.237%	(+)	3.60%	=	5.84%
DL Parent	DLPLUS	2.237%	(+)	4.60%	=	6.84%

Final Direct Loan Rates (July 1, 2015 and before July 1, 2016)

Note: See chapter 1 for further details and explanations.

I imagine that most parents would agree they should not have to pay an interest rate markup on parent PLUS loans that is more than double the markup charged the student borrower. This 4.66 percent parent add-on rate is nothing more than a mere first attempt estimate by Congress to accurately forecast the future costs associated with managing the new Federal Direct Loan Program, a program model enacted by Democratic legislative action and passed via the Health Care and Education Reconciliation Act of 2010. Now you, the parent, are largely asked to shoulder its weight and help guarantee its future solvency.

Federal Direct Parent PLUS loans accrue interest immediately upon full disbursement.

Deferment
"Why am I receiving a bill? My child is in school!"

The installment period begins within sixty days after the parent PLUS loan is fully disbursed.

As a parent borrower, you may elect to postpone payments on a Direct PLUS loan while your son or daughter attends school or during their six-month grace period after school.

In-School Deferment
This applies if you, the parent, return to school *or* if the dependent student whom the loan benefits attends school at least half-time (six credit hours as an undergraduate or eight credit hours as a graduate student in most cases).[71]

The in-school deferment option is perhaps the most tempting form of deferment for a parent borrower. It is also the most costly decision that you as a parent can make. Over the long run, the extra interest you will accrue if you elect this option for the four years that your son or daughter attends school can really add up.

Direct Parent PLUS loans do not receive an interest subsidy during periods of deferments. Example: Assume a parent borrows $7,000, fully disbursed at the beginning of each fall semester for a total of four years at a fixed interest rate of 7.21 percent.

The Prudent Parent
The prudent parent borrower satisfies the accrued interest every year.

	1st Disbursement $7,000.00	2nd Disbursement			
Freshman	i paid $504.70	$7,000.00	3rd Disbursement		
Sophomore	i paid $504.70	i paid $504.70	$7,000.00	4th Disbursement	
Junior	i paid $504.70	i paid $504.70	i paid $504.70	$7,000.00	
Senior	i paid $365.04	i paid $365.04	i paid $365.04	i paid $365.04	
Total i paid	$1,879.14	$1,374.44	$869.74	$365.04	**$4,488.36**
Payoff Bal.	$7,000.00	$7,000.00	$7,000.00	$7,000.00	**$28,000.00**

The first monthly installment under a ten-year standard fixed repayment schedule at 7.21% fixed interest is $328.14

The Procrastinator Parent

The procrastinator parent borrower postpones the interest payments and allows the interest to capitalize (add to the current balance) prior to initiating repayment.

	1st Disbursement $7,000.00	2nd Disbursement			
Freshman	$504.70	$7,000.00	3rd Disbursement		
Sophomore	$504.70	$504.70	$7,000.00	4th Disbursement	
Junior	$504.70	$504.70	$504.70	$7,000.00	
Senior	$365.04	$365.04	$365.04	$365.04	
Grace Period	$255.81	$255.81	$255.81	$255.81	
Outstanding i	$2,134.95	$1,630.25	$1,125.55	$620.85	
Payoff	$9,134.95	$8,630.25	$8,125.55	$7,620.85	**$33,511.60**

The first monthly installment under a ten-year standard fixed repayment schedule at 7.21% fixed interest is $392.73

Repayment

Under current congressional rules, your loan is automatically placed on a ten-year standard fixed repayment schedule once repayment begins. For most parents, the required monthly installment under the ten-year standard fixed repayment schedule is unaffordable. A most common remark among parent borrowers is "This installment bill reads more than my monthly mortgage payment." As a parent borrower, you do have alternative repayment schedules available. However, your choices are limited in number. Why so little flexibility in repayment plan choices for parents? The federal government wants you to pay it back most expeditiously. The sooner you pay back the money you borrowed, the less risk the federal government will have to undertake to raise money elsewhere—through ever larger US Treasury issuances.

Parent PLUS Loan Repayment Plan Selection Hierarchy

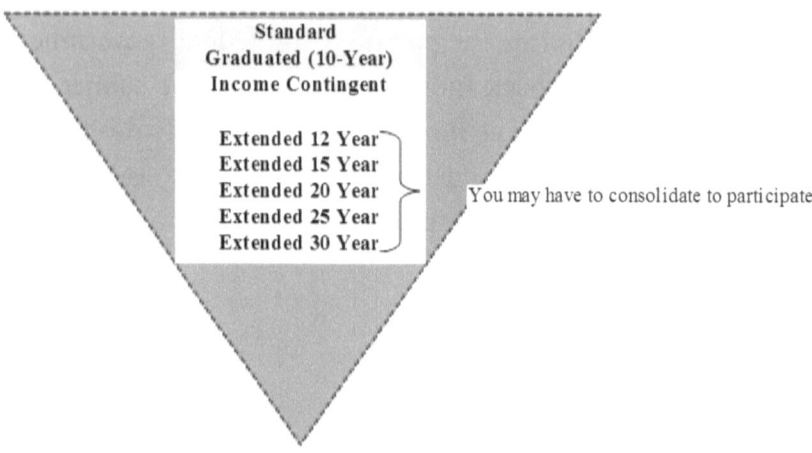

Extended Repayment Schedules

For the extended repayment schedules, your total loan portfolio balance is the biggest hurdle you must overcome in order to qualify to participate.

Extended Repayment Plan Minimum Loan Balance Eligibility Requirements

Minimum Loan Balance Requirements

>$7,500.00 - $10,000.00 - 12 year Extended Schedule
>$10,000.00 - $20,000.00 - 15 year
>$20,000.00 - $40,000.00 - 20 years
>$40,000.00 - $60,000.00 - 25 years
>$60,000.00 - 30 years

The second inconvenience is that not all assigned loan servicers offer all of these extended plan repayment selections. You must, therefore, engage your assigned loan servicer.

Income-Contingent Repayment (ICR)

Eligibility:
Direct Parent PLUS loans are eligible by way of direct consolidation if made after July 1, 2006.[72]

Note: If you are a holder of a FFEL Parent PLUS loan, you must create a Direct Consolidation loan to qualify.

Eligible Balance Requirements:
All eligible loan balances qualify.[73]

Loan Forgiveness:
Yes!
Forgiveness occurs on any balance that remains after twenty-five years of qualified payments (three hundred qualified monthly installment payments). Only a *partial* forgiveness of your loan balance is granted, however. You will be responsible to pay taxes on this forgiven balance. The tax rate imposed is your effective personal income tax rate at the time of forgiveness.

Do I qualify for Income-Contingent Repayment (ICR)?
Everyone who holds eligible loans should qualify.

What factors determine my monthly payment under the ICR plan?
- Total loan balance
- Adjusted gross income (AGI)
- Family size
- Tax filing status (individual, married filing jointly, married filing separately, head of household, etc.)

The steps to determine one's required payment are as follows:
Let's assume the parent borrower has an adjusted gross income (AGI) of $55,000, files taxes in 2015 as head of household, and has a family size of three—a parent and two dependent children.

1. Total the outstanding balance on all federal parent PLUS loans.

Loan Type	Loan Code	Payoff Balance
Direct Loan Plus – Parent (Child's senior year)	DLPLUS	$13,487.50
Direct Loan Plus – Parent (Child's junior year)	DLPLUS	$14,475.00
Direct Loan Plus – Parent (Child's sophomore year)	DLPLUS	$15,462.50
Direct Loan Plus – Parent (Child's freshman year)	DLPLUS	$16,540.00
		$59,965.00

2. Calculate the total monthly installment assuming a twelve-year fixed repayment schedule, using the following formula.

Loan Balance - $59,965
Interest Rate - 7.9%
Term (Years) - 12

$$\text{Monthly Payment} = \frac{\$59{,}965.00 \times 7.9/100/12}{1 - (1 - (1+7.9/100 \wedge 12 * 12 \text{ months}))}$$

$$= \$645.81$$

Or, in Excel, you may calculate the above as follows:

	Column A	B
Row 2	Current Balance	59,965.00
3	Rate	7.9
4	Term (Yrs)	12
5	Payment (Monthly)	=$B$2*($B$3/100/12)/(1-(1/(1+$B$3/100/12)^($B$4*12)))

The result is:

PARENT PLUS LOANS—"THANK YOU, MOM AND DAD!"

Loan Type	Payoff	i Rate	Term (Years)	Installment
DLPLUS – Parent	$13,487.50	7.90%	12	$145.26
DLPLUS – Parent	$14,475.00	7.90%	12	$155.89
DLPLUS – Parent	$15,462.50	7.90%	12	$166.53
DLPLUS – Parent	$16,540.00	7.90%	12	$178.13
Total	$59,965.00			$645.81

3. Locate the corresponding income percentage factor for 2015 that corresponds to an annual income level of $55,000 in the table below.

INCOME PERCENTAGE FACTOR for 2015			
Single		Married/Head of Household	
Income	Percentage Factor	Income	Percentage Factor
$11,150	55.00	$11,150	50.52
$15,342	57.79	$17,593	56.68
$19,741	60.57	$20,965	59.56
$24,240	66.23	$27,408	67.79
$28,537	71.89	$33,954	75.22
$33,954	80.33	$42,648	87.61
$42,648	88.77	$53,487	100.00
$53,488	100.00	$64,331	100.00
$64,331	100.00	$80,596	109.40
$77,318	111.80	$107,695	125.00
$99,003	123.50	$145,638	140.60
$140,221	141.20	$203,682	150.00
$160,776	150.00	$332,833	200.00
$286,370	200.00		

Source: Federal Register, vol. 80, no. 57. Wednesday, March 25, 2015/Notices www.ifap.cd.gov/fregisters/attachments/FR032515.pdf

Unfortunately, there is not an exact match for the income level of $55,000 in the table above. Therefore, we must us a method known as linear interpolation (steps four through nine).

4. Identify the nearest income entry that is less than $55,000 and the next highest income entry that is greater than $55,000. These dollar amounts are $53,487 and $64,331 respectively. Calculate their difference $64,331 - $53,487 = $10,844. This figure is referred to as the income interval at $10,844.

5. Locate the two income percentage factors for these two income levels and subtract their difference (same row, adjacent column, in the income percentage table above). The income percentage factor interval is: 100% - 100% = 0%.

6. Locate the closest income in the table that is less than the actual income and subtract this figure from the actual income of $55,000: $55,000 - $53,487 = $1,513.

7. Divide the result in step six by the income interval derived in step four: $1,513 ÷ $10,844 = .1395.

8. Multiply the result in step seven by the result in step five: .1395 x 0%. = 0%.

9. Add the result in step eight to the lower of the income percentage factors used in step five. The result is the income percentage factor (derived through linear interpolation): 0% + 100% = 100%. *(rounded to the nearest hundredth)*.

10. Multiply the twelve-year fixed monthly installment calculated in step two by the result in step nine: $645.81 x 100% = $645.81.

11. Calculate the borrower's discretionary income (discretionary income for the purpose of Income-Contingent Repayment is adjusted gross income [AGI] on the prior year's federal tax return minus the current year HHS Federal Poverty Guideline figure for a family size and State of residence, unadjusted at 100%). Multiply the result by 20 percent and divide by twelve (months): $55,000 - $20,090 = $34,910 x .20 = $6,982 ÷ 12 = $581.83.

PARENT PLUS LOANS—"THANK YOU, MOM AND DAD!"

| Form **1040** | Department of the Treasury—Internal Revenue Service (99) **U.S. Individual Income Tax Return** | 2015 | OMB No. 1545-0074 | IRS Use Only—Do not write or staple in this space. |

For the year Jan. 1–Dec. 31, 2015, or other tax year beginning _____ , 2015, ending _____ , 20 ___ | See separate instructions.

Your first name and initial | Last name | Your social security number

If a joint return, spouse's first name and initial | Last name | Spouse's social security number

Home address (number and street). If you have a P.O. box, see instructions. | Apt. no. | Make sure the SSN(s) above and on line 6c are correct.

City, town or post office, state, and ZIP code. If you have a foreign address, also complete spaces below (see instructions). | **Presidential Election Campaign** Check here if you, or your spouse if filing jointly, want $3 to go to this fund. Checking a box below will not change your tax or refund. ☐ You ☐ Spouse

Foreign country name | Foreign province/state/county | Foreign postal code

Filing Status
Check only one box.
1 ☐ Single
2 ☐ Married filing jointly (even if only one had income)
3 ☐ Married filing separately. Enter spouse's SSN above and full name here. ▶
4 ☐ Head of household (with qualifying person). (See instructions.) If the qualifying person is a child but not your dependent, enter this child's name here. ▶
5 ☐ Qualifying widow(er) with dependent child

Exemptions
6a ☐ **Yourself.** If someone can claim you as a dependent, **do not** check box 6a . . . . .
b ☐ **Spouse** . . . .
c **Dependents:**
(1) First name   Last name
(2) Dependent's social security number
(3) Dependent's relationship to you
(4) ✓ if child under age 17 qualifying for child tax credit (see instructions)

If more than four dependents, see instructions and check here ▶ ☐

Boxes checked on 6a and 6b ____
No. of children on 6c who:
• lived with you ____
• did not live with you due to divorce or separation (see instructions) ____
Dependents on 6c not entered above ____
Add numbers on lines above ▶ ____

d Total number of exemptions claimed . . . .

Income

Attach Form(s) W-2 here. Also attach Forms W-2G and 1099-R if tax was withheld.

If you did not get a W-2, see instructions.

7 Wages, salaries, tips, etc. Attach Form(s) W-2 . . . . | 7
8a Taxable interest. Attach Schedule B if required . . . . | 8a
b Tax-exempt interest. **Do not** include on line 8a . . . | 8b |
9a Ordinary dividends. Attach Schedule B if required . . . . | 9a
b Qualified dividends . . . . | 9b |
10 Taxable refunds, credits, or offsets of state and local income taxes . . . . . | 10
11 Alimony received . . . . | 11
12 Business income or (loss). Attach Schedule C or C-EZ . . . . | 12
13 Capital gain or (loss). Attach Schedule D if required. If not required, check here ▶ ☐ | 13
14 Other gains or (losses). Attach Form 4797 . . . . | 14
15a IRA distributions . | 15a | b Taxable amount . . . | 15b
16a Pensions and annuities | 16a | b Taxable amount . . . | 16b
17 Rental real estate, royalties, partnerships, S corporations, trusts, etc. Attach Schedule E | 17
18 Farm income or (loss). Attach Schedule F . . . . | 18
19 Unemployment compensation . . . . | 19
20a Social security benefits | 20a | b Taxable amount . . . | 20b
21 Other income. List type and amount _____ | 21
22 Combine the amounts in the far right column for lines 7 through 21. This is your **total income** ▶ | 22

Adjusted Gross Income

23 Educator expenses . . . . | 23
24 Certain business expenses of reservists, performing artists, and fee-basis government officials. Attach Form 2106 or 2106-EZ | 24
25 Health savings account deduction. Attach Form 8889 . . | 25
26 Moving expenses. Attach Form 3903 . . . . | 26
27 Deductible part of self-employment tax. Attach Schedule SE . | 27
28 Self-employed SEP, SIMPLE, and qualified plans . . | 28
29 Self-employed health insurance deduction . . . . | 29
30 Penalty on early withdrawal of savings . . . . . . | 30
31a Alimony paid   b Recipient's SSN ▶ _____ | 31a
32 IRA deduction . . . . | 32
33 Student loan interest deduction . . . . | 33
34 Tuition and fees. Attach Form 8917 . . . . | 34
35 Domestic production activities deduction. Attach Form 8903 | 35
36 Add lines 23 through 35 . . . . | 36
37 Subtract line 36 from line 22. This is your **adjusted gross income** . . . . . ▶ | 37

Line 37 Adjusted Gross Income (AGI)

For Disclosure, Privacy Act, and Paperwork Reduction Act Notice, see separate instructions. | Cat. No. 11320B | Form **1040** (2015)

INCOME PERCENTAGE FACTOR for 2016			
Single		Married/Head of Household	
Income	Percentage Factor	Income	Percentage Factor
$11,382	55.00	$11,382	50.52
$15,662	57.79	$17,959	56.68
$20,152	60.57	$21,402	59.56
$24,745	66.23	$27,979	67.79
$29,131	71.89	$34,661	75.22
$34,661	80.33	$43,536	87.61
$43,536	88.77	$54,601	100.00
$54,602	100.00	$65,671	100.00
$65,671	100.00	$82,275	109.40
$78,929	111.80	$109,938	125.00
$101,065	123.50	$148,672	140.60
$143,142	141.20	$207,925	150.00
$164,125	150.00	$339,766	200.00
$292,335	200.00		

12. The lesser of $581.83 or the result in step ten is your calculated monthly Income-Contingent Repayment (ICR) installment. The monthly Income-Contingent installment is $581.83.[74]

How may a parent PLUS loan borrower marry Income-Contingent Repayment (ICR) with Public Service Loan Forgiveness (PSLF)?

To participate in Income-Contingent Repayment as a parent borrower and holder of parent PLUS loans, who also seeks to participate in the Public Service Loan Forgiveness program (PSLF) as an employee of a government entity (federal, state, local or municipality) or a nonprofit (not-for-profit) 501(c)(3) organization, you must contact the Department of Education designated loan servicer to determine your eligibility.

Will I benefit?
It depends. Below are a few examples.

PARENT PLUS LOANS—"THANK YOU, MOM AND DAD!"

Key concept:
Income-Contingent Repayment (ICR) is more biased toward a combination of a lower outstanding loan balance relative to a higher income level.

Example 1:
Consider a hypothetical career police officer and his wife with a joint income of $85,000 and four dependent children. Two of the children attend college, and the other two children are in high school. The total outstanding parent PLUS debt is $80,000 and still growing.

Will this couple benefit? These are their loan repayment options (not limited to the following):

A monthly installment of $966.40 under a standard ten-year fixed repayment schedule at an assumed fixed interest rate of 7.9 percent.

A monthly installment of $581.44 under a thirty-year fixed repayment payment at an assumed fixed interest rate of 7.9 percent.

or

An Income-Contingent Repayment schedule combined with Public Service Loan Forgiveness (PSLF) participation will offer this couple the following:

The Math Explained:
Loan Balance is $80,000.00.

Calculate the total monthly installment assuming a twelve-year fixed repayment schedule = $861.58.
$107,695.00 - $80,596.00 = $27,099.00.
125.00% - 109.40% = 15.6% convert to .156.
$85,000.00 - $80,596.00 = $4,404.00.
$4,404 ÷ $27,099 = .16.
.156 x .16 = .02496 x 100 = 2.496%.
2.496% + 109.40 = 111.8 % (interpolated result for the income percentage factor).
$861.58 x 111.8% = $963.24 (no rounding)
$85,000.00 - $32,570.00 = $52,430.00.
$52,430.00 x .20 = $10,486.00.
$10,486.00 ÷ 12 = **$873.83**.

This couple's Income-Contingent Repayment (ICR) installment will require a payment of $873.83 (the lessor of the two calculations). If the police officer continues his full-time career providing public service while making 120 on-time qualified payments, any remaining loan balance is forgiven in just ten short years. A forgiveness balance is certain to remain since the ICR required payment of $873.83 falls well shy of the $966.40 per month payment necessary to satisfy the loan in ten years. The even greater PSLF benefit to this couple is delayed until the other two children graduate from college. Any parent PLUS loan balances necessary to fund their education will earn eligibility for public service loan forgiveness.

Example 2:
A hypothetical divorced mother of two college graduates struggles to meet her monthly payment obligation on her outstanding parent PLUS loan balance of $120,000.00, borrowed to pay her two daughters' college education. On a single income of

$45,000.00, this nonprofit professional employee with a family size of one faces a financial dilemma.

Will she benefit? These are her loan repayment options (not limited to the following):

A monthly installment of $1,449.60 under a standard ten-year fixed repayment schedule at an assumed fixed interest rate of 7.9 percent.

A monthly installment of $872.17 under an extended thirty-year fixed repayment schedule at an assumed fixed interest rate of 7.9 percent.

or

An Income-Contingent Repayment schedule combined with Public Service Loan Forgiveness (PSLF) participation will offer this mother the following:

The Math Explained:
Loan Balance = $120,000.00.
Twelve-year fixed repayment schedule monthly installment = $1,292.37.
$53,488.00 - $42,648.00 = $10,840.00.
100.00% - 88.7% = 11.3% convert to .113.
$45,000.00 - $42,648.00 = $2,352.00.
$2,352.00 ÷ $10,840.00 = .216.
.216 x .113 = .0244 x 100 = 2.44%.
2.44% + 100% = 102.44% (rounded to the nearest hundredth)
$1,292.37 x 102.44% = $1,323.90.

$45,000.00 - $11,770.00 = $33,230.00.
$33,230 x .20 = $6,646.00.
$6,646.00/12 = $553.83.

Yes, this single mother's ICR installment equals $553.83 (the lessor of the two calculations). If she remains consistent with her payments and commits to ten more years of public service, she will qualify for 100 percent loan forgiveness on any balance that remains. A forgiveness balance is certain to remain since the ICR required payment of $553.83 falls well shy of the $1,449.60 per month payment necessary to satisfy the loan in ten years.

Note: President Obama's 2015 Budget Proposal (published March 10, 2014) contained a request to cap the total amount of public service loan forgiveness at $57,500 for public sector employees. Congress never passed this budget.

CHAPTER 8

Direct Consolidation—Only If You Must!

"I'd like to consolidate my loans, please!"
[Response] "Why?"
"So I can lower my interest rate …"

—Anonymous

So you are thinking about consolidating your loans. Well, guess what? If you consolidate your federal loans, your new interest rate will be *higher* and with very few exceptions. Not much higher, but higher—higher by as much as one-eighth of 1 percent.[75] Do you welcome a higher rate of interest? Why then do millions of young borrowers eagerly make this decision to consolidate year in and year out as though the rules of simple finance need not apply to them? Perhaps, for these borrowers, the positives to consolidation outweigh the negatives. Let's explore this thought further: "Should I consolidate or should I not consolidate?"

Should I consolidate my loans?
Consolidation allows a borrower to convert and condense multiple individual loans (*only federal loans* are eligible) to one single, new loan.

Before consolidation, a sample federal student loan portfolio may look like this: (Hint: Sam's portfolio chapter 1, p.2. Yes, Sam may apply for consolidation of his loans and simultaneously apply for either an income-driven repayment plan or an extended repayment schedule, all at one-time, by simply completing an electronic application at the current Federal Student Aid website www.studentloans.gov. Sam may even apply prior to his grace period end date. Best of all, it's free!

Loan Type	Disbursement	Original Bal.	Current Bal.	*i* Rate	Outstanding *i*	Payoff
DLUNST	08/15/2014	$2,000.00	$2,000.00	4.66%	$114.25	$2,114.25
DLSTFD	08/15/2014	$5,500.00	$5,500.00	4.66%	$0.00	$5,500.00
DLUNST	08/18/2013	$2,000.00	$2,000.00	3.86%	$172.20	$2,172.20
DLSTFD	08/18/2013	$5,500.00	$5,500.00	3.86%	$106.72	$5,606.72
DLUNST	08/20/2012	$2,000.00	$2,000.00	6.80%	$438.45	$2,438.45
DLSTFD	08/20/2012	$4,500.00	$4,500.00	3.40%	$75.44	$4,575.44
DLUNST	08/15/2011	$2,000.00	$2,000.00	6.80%	$575.35	$2,575.35
DLSTFD	08/15/2011	$3,500.00	$3,500.00	3.40%	$0.00	$3,500.00
Total		$27,000.00	$27,000.00		$1,482.41	$28,482.41

After consolidation, this same federal student loan portfolio will appear like this:

Loan Type	Disbursement	Original Bal.	Current Bal.	*i* Rate	Outstanding *i*	Payoff
DLUCNS	11/15/2015	$9,300.25	$9,300.25	4.50%	$0.00	$9,300.25
DLSCNS	11/15/2015	$19,182.16	$19,182.16	4.50%	$0.00	19182.16
Totals		$28,482.41	$28,482.41			$28,482.41

Source: Federal Student Aid

Voila! Now you have ...
- One single loan
- One fixed interest rate
- One federal loan servicer (possibly a new servicer if you so choose)
- A new repayment schedule (from an expanded list of offerings)

- One monthly installment bill
- One transaction to make each month

But, even after consolidation, this one new loan will have two separate loan portions: an unsubsidized portion and a subsidized portion. For some hard-to-please borrowers, even this new condensed, two-line look is still a cosmetic disappointment. Sorry! The reason for this two-line segregation is simple. Suppose you decide to return to school or qualify for some other form of deferment period (i.e., unemployment, economic hardship, etc.). How else will your loan servicer be able to easily identify the subsidized portion of your loan portfolio (i.e., the government pays your interest)?

Consolidation may offer you additional extended repayment schedule choices.
For example, the loan portfolio presented above has a balance of $28,482.41. This portfolio balance may limit the borrower to only the standard ten-year repayment schedule or the graduated ten-year schedule. Unfortunately, to participate in the twenty-five-year extended or level repayment plan, a borrower must meet a minimum balance requirement of $30,000.00. This artificially forces the borrower to consider income-driven repayment (IDR) plans in an attempt to lower the payments. However, if the borrower's income is too high, the borrower may not be able to lower his or her installment below the ten-year schedule required payment. This borrower is cut out of participating in the twelve-year, twenty-year, twenty-five, or even thirty-year repayment plans. Why? The expanded menu of extended repayment plan options are essentially one-time selections made available to

borrowers mainly through the process of consolidation and based on certain minimum balance requirements below:

Consolidation Loan Extended Repayment Plan Balance Eligibility Requirements

Minimum Loan Balance Requirements

>$7,500.00 - $10,000.00 - 12 year Extended Schedule
>$10,000.00 - $20,000.00 - 15 year
>$20,000.00 - $40,000.00 - 20 years
>$40,000.00 - $60,000.00 - 25 years
>$60,000.00 - 30 years

Source: Federal Student Aid

If the above sample borrower portfolio was consolidated, this borrower could choose to participate in the twelve-year, the fifteen-year, or even the twenty-year repayment plans.

Consolidation will reset 100 percent of your entitled forbearance time.

Each loan issued to you is given up to three years of time that may be utilized during temporary periods of financial hardship. If you have been largely unfortunate early in the life of your loan(s), you may have exhausted most, if not all, of your deferment and forbearance options (i.e., unemployment deferment, general forbearance, and student loan debt burden forbearance, to list a few). The act of consolidation is simply the creation of a new loan. With this newly disbursed loan all your forbearance time is fully reloaded. That's right! Each three-year period of forbearance time is fully refreshed for you to use once again over the life of your new loan.

Consolidation may significantly soften the impact that a delinquency may have on your overall credit score.

Suppose you are delinquent on your student loan payments by a total of thirty days or more. You now run the risk of a delinquency being reported to the three major credit bureaus. Not a good thing if you are concerned about your credit score. Consider the sample portfolio above before consolidation occurred. This sample portfolio contained eight separately disbursed loans. For credit reporting purposes, each loan is separately reported to the three major credit bureaus. That's right! Eight separate delinquency reports will be generated for this one loan portfolio. If each delinquency report deducts ten to twenty points off your credit score per loan, this may potentially shave eighty- to 160 points off your credit score.). This may be repeated each and every month until the loan is brought current! By consolidating your loans, you can minimize the negative impact that a future delinquency may have on your credit report. Instead of eight separate loan delinquency reports, you will now only have one. This should limit the credit score deduction to only ten- to twenty-points for the entire loan portfolio. A big difference compared to the previous example.

Consolidation may allow you to remove a defaulted loan from collection status.

The act of consolidation is simply to pay off your old loan(s) with the issuance of a new loan. Consolidation will wipe out the loan(s) in default or debt management and create a brand-new loan with a clean credit history to build upon.

Consequences of default:
- I9 credit (installment debt is considered uncollectible)
- Reporting account balance(s) due in full
- Collection fees assessed
- Seizure of tax refund
- Garnishment of federal assistance
- Wage garnishment up to 15 percent
- No additional financial aid
- No repayment options
- Forfeiture of professional certification[76]

Should I *not* consolidate my loans?

Your new weighted average interest rate will be rounded up to the nearest one-eighth of a percentage point. Therefore, you will pay a higher rate of interest on your new consolidated loan. At best your new rate will be the same.

How do I calculate a weighted average interest rate?

Loan Type	Disbursement	Original Bal.	Current Bal.	i Rate	Outstanding i	Payoff
DLUNST	08/15/2014	$2,000.00	$2,000.00	4.66%	$114.25	$2,114.25
DLSTFD	08/15/2014	$5,500.00	$5,500.00	4.66%	$0.00	$5,500.00
DLUNST	08/18/2013	$2,000.00	$2,000.00	3.86%	$172.20	$2,172.20
DLSTFD	08/18/2013	$5,500.00	$5,500.00	3.86%	$106.72	$5,606.72
DLUNST	08/20/2012	$2,000.00	$2,000.00	6.80%	$438.45	$2,438.45
DLSTFD	08/20/2012	$4,500.00	$4,500.00	3.40%	$75.44	$4,575.44
DLUNST	08/15/2011	$2,000.00	$2,000.00	6.80%	$575.35	$2,575.35
DLSTFD	08/15/2011	$3,500.00	$3,500.00	3.40%	$0.00	$3,500.00
Total		$27,000.00	$27,000.00		$1,482.41	$28,482.41

Once again we refer to the sample loan portfolio (above):

Step 1: Find the portfolio weight for each loan in the portfolio.

Loan Type	Disbursement	Payoff Bal.	i Rate	Per Loan Weight Factor	Per Loan i Rate x Per Loan Weight Factor
Column A	B	C	D	E	F = D x E
DLUNST	08/15/2014	$2,114.25	4.66%	0.074	4.66 * .074 = .00346
DLSTFD	08/15/2014	$5,500.00	4.66%	0.193	4.66 * .193 = .00900
DLUNST	08/18/2013	$2,172.20	3.86%	0.076	3.86 * .076 = .00294
DLSTFD	08/18/2013	$5,606.72	3.86%	0.197	3.86 * .197 = .00760
DLUNST	08/20/2012	$2,438.45	6.80%	0.086	6.80 * .086 = .00582
DLSTFD	08/20/2012	$4,575.44	3.40%	0.161	3.40 * .161 = .00546
DLUNST	08/15/2011	$2,575.35	6.80%	0.090	6.80 * .090 = .00615
DLSTFD	08/20/2011	$3,500.00	3.40%	0.123	3.40 * .123 = .00418
Totals		$28,482.41		1.00	0.0446100

Source: Federal Student Aid

We determine each individual loan's weight to the overall portfolio by dividing each individual loan *payoff balance* (upon consolidation all outstanding interest is capitalized so we must use the current loan payoff balance and *not* the original loan balance or the current loan balance) by the total current portfolio payoff balance.
$2,114.25 ÷ $28,482.41 = .074.
$5,500.00 ÷ $28,482.41 = .193.
$2,172.20 ÷ $28,482.41 = .076.
$5,606.72 ÷ $28,482.41 = .197.
$2,438.45 ÷ $28,482.41 = .086.
$4,575.44 ÷ $28,482.41 = .161.
$2,575.35 ÷ $28,482.41 = .090.
$3,500.00 ÷ $28,482.41 = .123.

Step 2: Multiply each individual loan's weight by its respective interest rate at issuance.
.074 x .0466 = .00346.
.193 x .0466 = .00900.
.076 x .0386 = .00294.
.197 x .0386 = .00760.

.086 x .0680 = .00582.
.161 x .0340 = .00546.
.090 x .0680 = .00615.
.123 x .0340 = .00418.
Total = .04461 x 100 % = 4.461%.

Step 3: Round to the nearest higher one-eighth of 1 percent.[77] (Note: The nearest one-eighth of 1 percent is .125, .25, .375, .5, .625, .75, .875, or 1.0).

After rounding up, our new consolidation loan interest rate becomes 4.50%.

On a $50,000.00 consolidated loan, the above minor rounding effect will cost you approximately $112 in additional interest paid over a ten-year period of time, $252 in additional interest paid over a twenty-year period of time, or $333 in additional interest paid over a twenty-five-year period of time. Where is the value? You decide. Perform the calculation to your own portfolio and you be the judge as to whether or not consolidation benefits you. At best, your new weighted average interest rate after consolidation may stay the *same* (it will *never* be lower).

Consolidation may offer you additional repayment schedule choices. It may benefit you with negative credit reporting.

After consolidation, if your loan becomes delinquent, only one delinquency will be reported and not one for each separate loan. It may allow you to remove a defaulted loan from collection status prior to completion of a rehabilitation program.

CHAPTER 9

Your Credit Score— You Control It!

"I don't think I'm gonna pay this time around. They [the federal government] can come after me if they must. They know where they can find me. I'll just be sitting here on my fence post in my cowboy hat and my boots, just as I always am."

—Anonymous

What is a FICO score?
It is the most common credit score used by most lenders (i.e. banks) in the United States. A FICO score may range from a low of three hundred to a high of 850 points. The higher the score, the better your perceived credit risk to potential lenders. If you purchase a credit report on yourself, it is recommended that you purchase a FICO score report from one of the four major credit bureaus: Equifax, Experian, Innovis, or Trans Union.[78]

How is my credit score calculated?

Your FICO score considers data that is drawn from the four major credit bureaus and weighs each by its relevance through the use of proprietary software and mathematical formulas—formulas that are not published! The importance of each of these factors depends on where you lie on the life cycle: young, middle-aged, or aged. For most of us, our student loans will comprise the largest percentage of our indebtedness as we begin our adult life. Yes! Student loans are factored in your FICO score. And yes, your loan servicer will report your payment history to any of the four major credit bureaus.

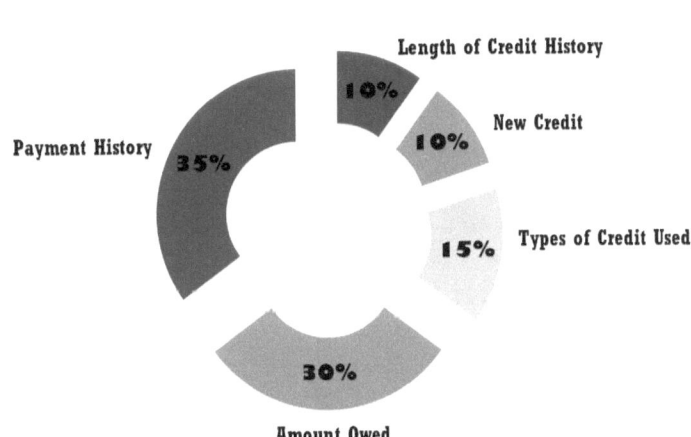

Although loan servicers have the *right* to report your repayment status *at any time within a given month,* most federal loan servicers will report you current until you become more than sixty days past due. This does not, however, relieve you from making consistent payments. If you miss, delay (through deferments or forbearances), or take advantage of paid-ahead statuses to postpone payments each month, don't be surprised to see your FICO or credit score drop.

CONCLUSION

How long until the US taxpayers proclaim, "We can't afford this either!"

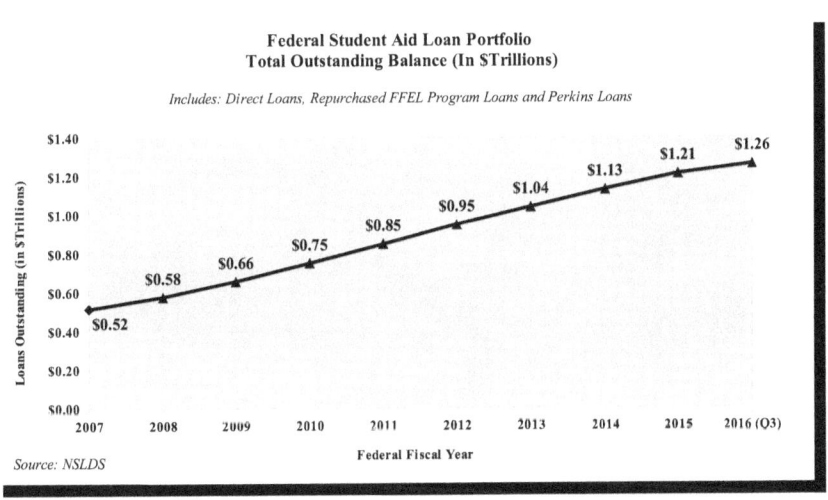

NOTES

1 US Bureau of the Census, *Current Population Survey, 2014 Annual Social & Economic Supplement*
2 https://studentaid.ed.gov
3 Ibid.
4 Ibid.
5 Bipartisan Student Loan Certainty Act of 2013, HR 1911. 113th Cong., 1st sess.
6 Ibid.
7 Ibid.
8 http://useconomy.about.com/od/fiscalpolicydefinitions/p/10-Year-Treasury.htm
9 World Bank, "Finding the Tipping Point—When Sovereign Debt Turns Bad," August 2010.
10 http://useconomy.about.com/od/fiscalpolicydefinitions/p/10-Year-Treasury.htm
11 http://money.cnn.com/news/economy/world_economies_gdp/
12 http://newyorkfed.org/markets/pridealers_current.html
13 http://www.ed.gov
14 http://studentaid.ed.gov
15 Ibid.
16 http://www.ed.gov
17 https://studentaid.ed.gov
18 Ibid.
19 Ibid.
20 Ibid.
21 Ibid.
22 Ibid.
23 Ibid.
24 Ibid.
25 Ibid.

26 Ibid.
27 Ibid.
28 Ibid.
29 Ibid.
30 Ibid.
31 Ibid.
32 Ibid.
33 Ibid.
34 Ibid
35 Ibid.
36 Ibid.
37 Ibid.
38 Ibid.
39 Ibid.
40 http://www.ed.gov
41 Ibid
42 Ibid
43 Ibid
44 Ibid
45 https://studentaid.gov/publicservice
46 Ibid
47 https://whitehouse.gov
48 https://studentaid.gov/publicservice
49 Ibid
50 Ibid
51 Ibid
52 https://studentaid.gov/publicservice
53 Ibid.
54 Ibid.
55 Ibid.
56 Ibid.
57 https://studentaid.ed.gov
58 Ibid.
59 Ibid.
60 Ibid.
61 Ibid.
62 http://www.ed.gov
63 Ibid.
64 Ibid.
65 Ibid.
66 Ibid.

67 Ibid.
68 Ibid.
69 Ibid.
70 Ibid.
71 Ibid.
72 Ibid.
73 https://studentaid.ed.gov
74 Ibid.
75 https://www.ed.gov
76 Ibid
77 Ibid.
78 Don Lemoine and Craig Taylor, eds., *Financial Planning: Process and Environment*, 3rd ed. (The American College Press, 2009), 8.44.

www.ingramcontent.com/pod-product-compliance
Lightning Source LLC
Chambersburg PA
CBHW021954170526
45157CB00003B/980